Anatomy of the R Scam

Vol. 1 in the series:

"Defeating Common Scams with Common Sense!"

(An expository exegesis concerning a variety of themes)

by

Hon. T Mitchell, DD, PhD

E-Heart Broken by a Lost Love

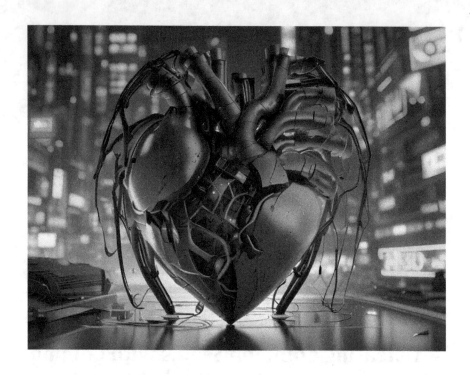

Original Artwork by Author

*Produced with Photo Director 365
on Windows 10 Enterprise*

B

D

Front Matter

"Anatomy of the Romance Scam" is an eye-opening non-fiction book that delves into the intricate workings of one of the most prevalent and devastating forms of cybercrime – the romance scam. With astonishing statistics revealing millions of individuals falling victim to this heartless deception each year, this book aims to shed light on the mechanics behind these scams, their psychological tactics, and the lasting consequences they have on their victims.

Through meticulous research and interviews with survivors, experts, and law enforcement officials, "Anatomy of the Romance Scam" unravels the hidden world of online fraudsters who exploit emotions to gain personal and financial advantages. From initial contact on dating websites or social media platforms to the elaborate manipulation techniques employed during the scam, readers will embark on a journey through real-life stories that showcase the devastating impact this fraud has on unsuspecting individuals.

The book explores the psychological tactics utilized by scammers, such as love bombing, mirroring, and gaslighting, to establish trust and exploit vulnerabilities. It also investigates the increasingly sophisticated methods employed by criminals, including the use of stolen identities, fake profiles, and advanced technology to create a convincing facade. By dissecting actual cases, readers will gain crucial insights into the red flags to watch out for and learn how to protect themselves and their loved ones from falling victim to these deceitful schemes.

Beyond exposing the modus operandi of romance scammers, "Anatomy of the Romance Scam" delves deep into the aftermath experienced by survivors. It examines the emotional turmoil, financial ruin, and oftentimes shattered self-esteem that victims face after being deceived by someone they believed was their soulmate. Offering guidance and resources for recovery, this book aims to empower victims by providing tools to rebuild their lives and regain confidence.

E

Ultimately, "Anatomy of the Romance Scam" serves as a wake-up call for both those seeking love online and society as a whole. By highlighting the vulnerabilities within our digital landscape and offering practical advice for prevention and support, this book aspires to foster awareness, resilience, and ultimately eradicate this insidious crime that preys on individuals' longing for love and companionship.

F

Table of Contents

Original Artwork by Author   A

Copyright 2024   C

Front Matter   E

Table of Contents   G

Introduction: The Rise of the Romance Scam   1

Understanding the Psychology of Online Deception   9

Analysis of the role trust plays in online relationships and how scammers manipulate this trust: 15

Love Bombing: The Art of Seduction   17

Building Trust and Intimacy   21

Mirroring: Creating an Illusion of Compatibility 27

Gaslighting: Manipulating Reality and Emotions 35

Identification of common signs and behaviors that may indicate gaslighting in an online relationship: 40

Unveiling the Scammers: Profiles, Identities, and Facades   44

The Mechanics of Online Connections: Dating Websites and Social Media Platforms   52

Red Flags and Warning Signs: How to Spot a Romance Scam   60

Resources and guidance for reporting suspected scams and seeking help: 66

Real-Life Stories: Tales of Deception and Betrayal   68

Personal Accounts from Survivors: 70

Emotional Journey and Impact: 72

Insights for Prevention and Empowerment: 76

Consequences: Emotional, Financial, and Psychological Fallout 78

Analyzing the financial implications for victims: 80

Exploring coping mechanisms and support for victims: 84

Practical Steps and Guidance for Recovering from the Emotional, Financial, and Psychological Fallout 86

Resources for Emotional Support: 88

G

Practical Steps for Recovery: 92

Prevention and Global Efforts: Combating the Romance Scam   96

Safe online dating practices are also crucial in preventing romance scams. Follow these guidelines: 100

Calls to Action: Taking a Stand Against Romance Scams   104

H

Introduction: The Rise of the Romance Scam

Romance scams have become an increasingly prevalent form of cybercrime, targeting individuals seeking love and companionship online. These scams can take various forms, ranging from fraudulent profiles on dating websites to manipulative tactics on social media platforms. Understanding the concept and prevalence of romance scams is crucial in raising awareness and preventing further victimization.

Romance scams typically involve individuals creating fake personas or profiles to deceive unsuspecting victims. They prey on the vulnerability and desires of individuals searching for love and companionship. The internet provides scammers with the perfect platform to manipulate emotions, establish trust, and exploit personal and financial vulnerabilities.

Online dating platforms are a common breeding ground for romance scams. Scammers create attractive profiles using stolen photos and false information to lure in potential victims. They may engage in conversations and build relationships over time, gradually gaining the trust and affection of their targets. Social media platforms also offer scammers an avenue to initiate contact, often through friend requests or direct messages.

The rise of romance scams can be attributed to several factors. The anonymity offered by online platforms allows scammers to operate with minimal risk of detection or consequence. Additionally, the global reach of the internet provides a vast pool of potential victims from all walks of life. The ease of creating fake identities further contributes to the proliferation of these scams.

To combat romance scams effectively and protect potential victims, it is essential to recognize the signs and tactics employed by scammers. Awareness and education play a pivotal role in preventing individuals from falling victim to manipulation and deception. By understanding the mechanics behind romance scams, individuals can be more cautious when engaging in online relationships.

This chapter provides an overview of romance scams, explaining their prevalence in today's digital landscape. It aims to shed light on the different forms they can take, including scams originating from online dating platforms and social media interactions. By familiarizing ourselves with the methods used by scammers, we can better equip ourselves against their deceitful tactics and work towards eradicating this form of cybercrime.

In the following chapters, we will delve deeper into the psychological tactics employed by romance scammers, explore real-life stories from survivors, and provide guidance on prevention, recovery, and rebuilding after becoming a victim. Together, let us strive to raise awareness and foster resilience against romance scams, ensuring a safer digital environment for all individuals seeking love and companionship online.

Statistics and data play a crucial role in understanding the magnitude of the romance scam problem and the need for awareness and prevention. Each year, millions of individuals fall victim to romance scams, resulting in devastating emotional, financial, and psychological consequences. By presenting compelling statistics and data, this chapter aims to shed light on the scale of the issue and emphasize the importance of addressing it.

According to recent studies, romance scams are one of the most prevalent forms of cybercrime globally. In the United States alone, the Federal Trade Commission reported over 23,000 complaints related to romance scams in 2020, with losses exceeding $300 million. These numbers only represent reported cases, indicating that the actual number of victims could be significantly higher due to underreporting.

Furthermore, research indicates that romance scams are not limited to specific demographics or geographical regions. People from all walks of life, across different age groups and socio-economic backgrounds, have fallen prey to these deceptive schemes. It is a problem that transcends borders, affecting individuals worldwide.

The financial impact of romance scams is staggering. Victims often lose substantial amounts of money, sometimes their entire life savings, as scammers exploit their emotions and manipulate them into providing financial assistance. Reports show that the average amount lost by victims in a romance scam ranges from several thousand dollars to tens of thousands.

Beyond the financial aspect, romance scams take a significant toll on victims' emotional well-being. The betrayal experienced when they discover that their supposed soulmate was a fraud can cause severe emotional distress, leading to feelings of shame, guilt, anger, and heartbreak. Many victims also suffer from long-lasting psychological effects, such as trust issues and self-doubt.

It is worth noting that romance scams are vastly underreported due to the stigma and embarrassment associated with falling victim to such scams. Many individuals feel ashamed or blame themselves for being deceived, leading them to keep their experiences a secret. This underreporting further highlights the urgency and necessity of raising awareness about romance scams.

By presenting these statistics and data, we aim to highlight the widespread nature of romance scams and emphasize the need for awareness and prevention efforts. It is crucial for individuals to educate themselves about the red flags and warning signs of romance scams and understand the tactics employed by scammers. Awareness campaigns, educational programs, and collective action are essential in combating this insidious crime that preys upon people's longing for love and companionship.

Together, we can work towards eradicating romance scams and protecting potential victims from experiencing the devastating consequences inflicted by these heartless criminals.

Romance scammers operate with various motives and employ a range of tactics to deceive their victims. Understanding their mindset and motivations is crucial in recognizing the red flags and protecting oneself from falling victim to these scams.

First and foremost, romance scammers are driven by financial gain. They exploit the emotions and vulnerabilities of their victims to extract money or valuable assets. Their ultimate goal is to manipulate victims into sending them funds under false pretenses, often by creating a false sense of urgency or appealing to their victims' desire for love and companionship. By appearing as sympathetic figures in need, such as individuals claiming to be overseas military personnel or victims of tragic circumstances, scammers exploit their victims' empathy and generosity.

Another motive behind romance scams is personal gratification. Scammers derive pleasure from the act of deceiving others, exerting control over their emotions and manipulating their trust. They enjoy the power they hold over their victims and take satisfaction in successfully carrying out their fraudulent schemes.

To accomplish their objectives, romance scammers rely on a variety of manipulative tactics. Love bombing is a common strategy where scammers shower their targets with excessive affection, attention, and flattery in an attempt to create a sense of intimacy and trust. They exploit their victims' longing for love and use it as a weapon against them.

Manipulation plays a significant role in romance scams, with scammers employing psychological techniques to exploit their victims' emotions. They may use guilt or shame to coerce victims into complying with their demands or entice them into compromising situations. Additionally, scammers often employ gaslighting, a tactic that involves distorting the truth or making victims doubt their own experiences and perceptions. This manipulative technique is used to control victims and keep them trapped within the scam.

Exploitation of emotions is also a key tactic utilized by romance scammers. They prey on individuals who are seeking genuine connections and exploit their vulnerability for personal gain. By mirroring their victims' interests, values, and beliefs, scammers create an illusion of compatibility and forge a deep emotional connection. This emotional investment makes it difficult for victims to see through the deception until it is too late.

In conclusion, understanding the motives and tactics of romance scammers is vital in protecting oneself from becoming a victim. Recognizing manipulation, being aware of the signs of love bombing, and maintaining a skeptical mindset when engaging in online relationships can help individuals avoid falling prey to these deceitful schemes. By shedding light on the mindset and tactics of romance scammers, we can empower ourselves and others to stay vigilant against this prevalent form of cybercrime.

The devastating impact of romance scams on their victims cannot be overstated. Beyond the financial loss, there is a profound emotional toll that individuals experience after being deceived by someone they believed was their romantic partner. The aftermath of a romance scam can result in long-lasting psychological and emotional consequences that require extensive healing and support.

Emotionally, victims of romance scams often find themselves grappling with a range of complex emotions. They may experience shock and disbelief upon discovering that the person they thought they knew and loved was nothing more than an elaborate fabrication. The betrayal and violation of trust can lead to feelings of profound sadness, anger, and even self-blame for falling victim to the scam. Victims may also struggle with a sense of shame or embarrassment, as they grapple with the realization that they were manipulated and deceived.

Financially, the impact of romance scams can be devastating. Many victims lose significant amounts of money to scammers who exploit their emotions and trust. They may be coerced into sending funds for various reasons, such as medical emergencies, travel expenses, or investments that promise high returns. These financial losses can strip victims of their savings, retirement accounts, and even push them into bankruptcy. The ripple effects extend beyond the immediate financial strain, often causing long-term financial instability and difficulties.

Psychologically, the aftermath of a romance scam can be overwhelming. Victims may experience symptoms akin to post-traumatic stress disorder (PTSD), including anxiety, depression, panic attacks, and nightmares. The trauma of being deceived by someone they thought loved them leaves lasting scars on their mental well-being. Additionally, victims may develop trust issues and have difficulty forming new relationships due to the fear of being hurt again. The toll on their self-esteem and self-worth can be profound, as they question their judgment and ability to navigate future relationships.

The challenges faced by romance scam victims should not be underestimated, but it is essential to emphasize that recovery is possible. With the support of counseling services, therapy, and resources tailored to their specific needs, survivors can begin the healing process. Rebuilding one's life after a romance scam involves reclaiming personal power, learning to trust again, and developing strategies to protect oneself from future scams. It requires patience, self-compassion, and an understanding that recovery takes time.

In conclusion, the impact of romance scams on their victims is far-reaching and multifaceted. The emotional trauma, financial loss, and psychological consequences experienced by individuals who fall victim to these scams cannot be ignored. It is crucial for society to acknowledge the severity of these crimes and work towards creating awareness, prevention strategies, and support systems for survivors. By doing so, we can help victims regain their confidence, rebuild their lives, and prevent others from suffering similar fates.

The final part of this chapter emphasizes the importance of raising awareness about romance scams among individuals, communities, law enforcement agencies, and governments. It highlights the need for collective action to combat this form of cybercrime and protect potential victims.

Raising awareness about romance scams is crucial in preventing more individuals from falling victim to these deceptive schemes. By educating the public about the tactics and methods employed by scammers, we can empower individuals to recognize the warning signs and protect themselves and their loved ones.

Communities play a vital role in spreading awareness and creating a support network for potential victims. Through community outreach programs, workshops, and educational campaigns, we can inform people about the risks associated with online relationships and provide resources for prevention and recovery.

Law enforcement agencies also have a responsibility to address romance scams. By allocating resources to investigate and prosecute scammers, they send a strong message that this type of fraudulent activity will not be tolerated. Collaboration between law enforcement agencies across borders is essential in combating the global nature of romance scams.

Furthermore, governments can take action by enacting legislation and regulations that specifically target romance scams. By implementing stricter measures against scammers and providing support for victims, governments can contribute to the overall effort of preventing and addressing this form of cybercrime.

In conclusion, raising awareness about romance scams is crucial in combating this prevalent and devastating form of cybercrime. By working together as individuals, communities, law enforcement agencies, and governments, we can create a safer digital landscape and protect potential victims from falling prey to these deceitful schemes.

Understanding the Psychology of Online Deception

Individuals seeking love and companionship online are vulnerable to a variety of psychological tactics employed by romance scammers. These scammers exploit the natural desire for connection and companionship, preying on the emotional needs and longing for love that many individuals have.

One factor that makes individuals vulnerable to online deception in romantic relationships is the desire for connection and companionship. In today's digital age, many people turn to online dating websites and social media platforms to find potential partners. They may feel lonely or isolated, hoping to find someone who understands and accepts them. Scammers take advantage of these vulnerabilities by creating fake profiles and presenting themselves as the perfect match. They offer an escape from loneliness and the promise of a loving relationship.

Another vulnerability that scammers exploit is the emotional needs and longing for love that individuals have. Scammers are skilled at using emotional manipulation techniques to establish trust and dependency. They may shower their victims with flattery, validation, and empathy, making them feel special and loved. By creating a false sense of intimacy and emotional connection, scammers manipulate their victims into believing they have found true love.

Cognitive biases also play a role in making individuals susceptible to online deception. Confirmation bias, for example, can lead individuals to overlook warning signs and red flags in their online relationships because they want to believe that they have found a genuine connection. Sunk cost fallacy may also come into play, causing victims to continue investing time, money, and emotions into a relationship even when there are clear signs of deceit.

Loneliness, insecurity, and low self-esteem are additional vulnerabilities that scammers exploit. Individuals who are feeling lonely or insecure may be more likely to seek validation and acceptance from others. Scammers capitalize on these feelings, offering reassurance, attention, and affection. Falling victim to a romance scam can further damage victims' self-perception and self-worth, as they may blame themselves for being deceived.

Trust plays a crucial role in online relationships, and scammers manipulate this trust to their advantage. Victims often hesitate to question or doubt their online partner's authenticity because they have invested time, emotions, and sometimes even money into the relationship. Scammers know this and use it to their advantage by exploiting the trust that has been established. Developing healthy skepticism and maintaining a balance between trust and caution is essential when engaging in online connections.

Overall, understanding the vulnerabilities within online relationships is crucial in recognizing the tactics used by romance scammers. By being aware of these vulnerabilities and the emotional manipulation techniques employed by scammers, individuals can better protect themselves from falling prey to these deceitful schemes. It is important to approach online relationships with caution and skepticism while also seeking genuine connections built on trust and mutual respect.

Emotional manipulation techniques play a crucial role in the success of romance scams. Scammers are skilled at exploiting vulnerabilities and manipulating emotions to establish trust and dependency. In this section, we will explore the various psychological tactics used by scammers to deceive their victims.

One common technique employed by scammers is flattery. They shower their victims with compliments, making them feel special, desirable, and loved. By appealing to their ego and creating a sense of validation, scammers quickly establish a positive emotional connection. Victims may feel a surge of excitement and happiness, believing that they have finally found their soulmate. However, it is essential to recognize that these flattering words are often insincere and designed to manipulate emotions.

Another tactic that scammers employ is validation. They take the time to listen and understand their victims' desires, fears, and dreams. By providing a sympathetic ear, scammers create an illusion of empathy and understanding. Victims may feel a deep emotional connection, believing that they have found someone who truly cares about them. This validation creates a powerful bond between the scammer and the victim, making it

10

increasingly difficult for the victim to question the authenticity of the relationship.

Empathy is another effective tool used by scammers to manipulate emotions. They mimic their victims' feelings and emotions, making them believe that they have found someone who understands them on a profound level. Scammers are skilled at mirroring their victims' emotional state, ensuring that they appear supportive, compassionate, and trustworthy. This emotional connection makes it challenging for victims to doubt the sincerity of their online partner.

Scammers go to great lengths to create a false sense of intimacy and emotional connection with their victims. They use tactics such as sharing personal stories, disclosing vulnerabilities, and expressing deep affection. By engaging in intimate conversations, scammers elicit feelings of trust and openness in their victims. This false intimacy fuels the belief that the relationship is genuine and further strengthens the emotional bond.

It's important to note that these emotional manipulation techniques are not exclusive to romance scams. They are commonly used in other forms of manipulation and deception as well. By understanding these tactics, individuals can become more informed and skeptical when engaging in online relationships.

In conclusion, scammers employ various psychological tactics to manipulate their victims' emotions in romance scams. Techniques like flattery, validation, empathy, and creating a false sense of intimacy all contribute to establishing trust and dependency. By recognizing these manipulation techniques, individuals can protect themselves from falling victim to romance scams and maintain a healthy skepticism in online relationships.

Cognitive biases play a significant role in online relationships, often leading individuals to overlook warning signs and red flags. Understanding these biases and learning to overcome them is crucial in making more informed decisions and protecting oneself from romance scams.

One common cognitive bias in online relationships is confirmation bias. This bias occurs when individuals actively seek out information that confirms their preexisting beliefs or desires. In the context of romance scams, victims may ignore or dismiss warning signs because they want to believe that the person they have met online is genuine and trustworthy. They may selectively focus on positive interactions and experiences while disregarding any inconsistencies or suspicious behavior.

Another bias that can cloud judgment in online relationships is the sunk cost fallacy. This bias arises when individuals continue to invest time, emotions, or resources into a situation based on the belief that they have already invested too much to give up. In romance scams, victims may feel reluctant to end the relationship or question their online partner's authenticity because they have already invested considerable time, effort, and emotions into the connection. They may believe that ending the relationship would mean admitting defeat or feeling embarrassed about being deceived.

Recognizing and overcoming these cognitive biases is essential for making rational decisions in online relationships. One effective strategy is to seek objective perspectives and feedback from trusted friends or family members who may offer a more detached viewpoint. By sharing their concerns and observations, these individuals can help highlight any inconsistencies or red flags that might be overlooked due to confirmation bias.

Additionally, taking a step back and evaluating the relationship from an outside perspective can provide valuable insights. This can involve questioning one's own motivations, intentions, and emotional investment in the relationship. By critically examining the evidence and considering alternative explanations for any suspicious behavior or inconsistencies, individuals can mitigate the influence of cognitive biases.

It is also essential to maintain a healthy skepticism when engaging in online relationships. While trust is important, it should be balanced with caution and critical thinking. Individuals should be mindful of their own vulnerability to cognitive biases and actively question information that seems too good to be true or contradicts previous knowledge or experiences.

In conclusion, cognitive biases significantly impact judgment in online relationships. Confirmation bias and the sunk cost fallacy can lead individuals to overlook warning signs and red flags associated with romance scams. Recognizing these biases and actively working to overcome them through seeking objective perspectives, evaluating the relationship critically, and maintaining a healthy skepticism can help individuals make more informed decisions and protect themselves from falling victim to online deception.

During the course of a romance scam, perpetrators often target individuals who are experiencing feelings of loneliness, insecurity, and low self-esteem. These emotional vulnerabilities make victims more susceptible to manipulation and deception.

Scammers are skilled at identifying and exploiting these weaknesses for their personal gain. They understand that individuals who are lonely or lacking in self-confidence may be more willing to seek connection and affirmation from an online relationship. By playing into these insecurities, scammers create a sense of dependence and trust with their victims.

The tactics used by scammers to exploit these vulnerabilities can vary, but they often involve showering the victim with attention, affection, and compliments. Through constant flattery and validation, scammers are able to boost the victim's self-esteem and make them feel valued and desired.

By preying on feelings of loneliness, scammers create an illusion of companionship and understanding. They provide a sympathetic ear and offer support for any emotional struggles the victim may be facing. This emotional connection is carefully cultivated to make the victim believe that they have found a genuine soulmate.

The impact of falling victim to a romance scam can be devastating for an individual's self-perception and self-worth. Discovering that the relationship they believed was real was actually based on deceit can lead to feelings of shame, embarrassment, and self-blame. Victims may question their judgment and feel foolish for having trusted someone who turned out to be a fraud.

Additionally, the financial loss often associated with romance scams can further damage a victim's sense of self-worth. They may feel financially irresponsible or blame themselves for not recognizing the signs of deception earlier. This combination of emotional and financial harm can have long-lasting effects on a person's overall well-being.

13

It is crucial to recognize the tactics employed by scammers to exploit these vulnerabilities. By understanding how scammers manipulate individuals through emotional manipulation, we can empower ourselves and others to recognize the signs of a romance scam. It's important to remember that falling victim to a scam does not reflect our worth as individuals; it is simply a result of calculated manipulation by skilled criminals.

By raising awareness about the psychological tactics used by romance scammers, we can help individuals build resilience and develop healthy skepticism when engaging in online relationships. It is essential to prioritize our emotional well-being and maintain a balanced perspective when interacting with others online, especially when vulnerable emotions come into play.

In the next section, we will delve deeper into the role of trust in online deception and explore strategies for maintaining a healthy level of caution while fostering genuine connections in the digital world.

Analysis of the role trust plays in online relationships and how scammers manipulate this trust:

Trust is a fundamental aspect of any relationship, including those established online. In the context of romance scams, trust plays a crucial role in enabling scammers to exploit their victims. Scammers are skilled at creating a facade of trustworthiness and authenticity, often manipulating their victims into believing in their sincerity and genuine intentions.

One reason why victims may hesitate to question or doubt their online partner's authenticity is the emotional investment they have made in the relationship. When individuals develop feelings for someone they have met online, they are often more inclined to trust and believe in that person's words and actions. This emotional investment can cloud judgment and make it difficult for victims to see the warning signs that something might be amiss.

Scammers take advantage of this emotional connection by carefully crafting their stories and personas to evoke empathy and trust. They often go to great lengths to create convincing backstories, complete with photos, personal details, and even fake social media profiles, all aimed at building trust with their victims. By posing as someone who appears reliable and trustworthy, scammers exploit their victims' natural inclination to trust.

Additionally, victims may feel hesitant to question their online partner's authenticity due to fear of losing the relationship. Romance scams often evolve over time, with scammers investing weeks or months in developing the relationship before revealing their true intentions. This gradual progression gives victims a false sense of security and makes it harder for them to question or doubt their partner's authenticity.

To develop a healthy skepticism and maintain a balance between trust and caution in online connections, it is essential to be aware of the tactics scammers use to manipulate trust. Educating oneself about common red flags and warning signs of romance scams can help individuals identify potential deception early on.

It is also important to verify information independently and conduct thorough research on the person claiming to be a romantic partner. This can involve reverse image searches, verifying social media profiles, and cross-checking details provided by the individual. By taking these steps, one can minimize the risk of falling victim to a romance scam.

Furthermore, seeking advice from trusted friends or family members can provide an outside perspective on the relationship and help identify any inconsistencies or suspicious behavior. Trusted individuals may be more objective in assessing the situation and can offer valuable insights.

Ultimately, maintaining a healthy level of skepticism while still being open to new connections is key in online relationships. While trust is an important foundation for any relationship, it is crucial to strike a balance by being cautious and attentive to potential signs of deception. By remaining vigilant, individuals can protect themselves from falling victim to the manipulative tactics employed by romance scammers.

Love Bombing: The Art of Seduction

Love bombing is a manipulative tactic used by romance scammers to establish trust and control over their victims. It involves showering the victim with excessive affection, attention, and flattery in order to create an intense emotional bond. By bombarding the victim with love and affection, scammers aim to disarm their skepticism and exploit their desire for love and companionship.

The concept of love bombing can be best understood through examples and case studies that highlight the various techniques and strategies employed by scammers. These examples serve as cautionary tales, illustrating the devastating impact love bombing can have on unsuspecting individuals.

One common technique used in love bombing is an overwhelming display of affection and compliments. Scammers often bombard their victims with messages professing their love and admiration from the very beginning of the relationship. These messages may appear romantic and genuine, but they are carefully crafted to manipulate the victim's emotions. The scammer aims to create a sense of euphoria and infatuation, making the victim more susceptible to their manipulation.

Another technique used in love bombing is rapid escalation of the relationship. Scammers may push for quick commitment or marriage, claiming that they have found their soulmate in the victim. This accelerated pace creates a false sense of intimacy and connection, leading the victim to believe that they have met their perfect match. However, this rapid progression is solely aimed at gaining control over the victim's emotions and decision-making processes.

Furthermore, scammers often exploit vulnerabilities and insecurities to build a deep emotional bond with their victims. They may listen attentively to the victim's problems, offer unwavering support, and provide a shoulder to lean on. By creating an illusion of understanding and compassion, scammers manipulate their victims into believing that they have found a rare connection based on trust and empathy.

It is essential for individuals to be able to identify signs of love bombing in order to protect themselves from falling victim to romance scams. Some

17

red flags to watch out for include excessive flattery, declarations of love too soon in the relationship, and intense expressions of affection. When these signs are present, it is important to approach the relationship with caution and skepticism.

Recovering from the effects of love bombing can be a long and challenging process. Victims may experience a loss of self-esteem, confusion, and emotional turmoil after realizing they have been manipulated. It is crucial for survivors to seek support from friends, family, or professionals who can provide guidance and help them heal from the emotional trauma.

In conclusion, love bombing is a manipulative tactic employed by romance scammers to establish trust and control over their victims. By understanding how love bombing works and being able to identify its signs, individuals can protect themselves from falling prey to these deceitful schemes. Remember that genuine love takes time to develop and is built on mutual trust and respect.

Emotional manipulation lies at the heart of love bombing, the deceptive technique utilized by romance scammers. By exploiting victims' desires for affection and attention, scammers are able to establish control and manipulate their emotions.

One of the primary emotional manipulation techniques employed in love bombing is excessive flattery. Scammers shower their victims with compliments and praise, making them feel special and desired. This constant stream of positive reinforcement creates a sense of validation and boosts victims' self-esteem. As a result, victims become emotionally dependent on the scammer's approval and affection.

Another common technique used in love bombing is the rapid progression of the relationship. Scammers often push for intimate conversations and declarations of love early on, effectively accelerating the emotional connection between themselves and their victims. This whirlwind romance can be overwhelming for victims, clouding their judgment and preventing them from recognizing red flags or inconsistencies in the scammer's story.

Scammers also employ intense expressions of affection as a means of manipulating victims' emotions. This can include lavish gifts, surprise visits, and constant declarations of love. By bombarding victims with these displays of affection, scammers create an illusion of a deep and meaningful connection. Victims may interpret these actions as genuine gestures of love, further blurring the lines between reality and manipulation.

The impact of these emotional manipulation techniques on victims' emotions and decision-making processes is significant. Love bombing can lead victims to develop strong feelings of attachment and dependency on the scammer. Victims often find it difficult to question or doubt the scammer's intentions due to the intense emotions they have been subjected to.

Additionally, love bombing can impair victims' ability to make rational decisions. The emotional intensity created by scammers leaves victims vulnerable to manipulation and coercion, which can result in financial exploitation or other harmful consequences. Victims may choose to overlook warning signs or red flags in favor of maintaining the illusion of a perfect relationship that has been carefully orchestrated by the scammer.

Understanding the emotional manipulation techniques used in love bombing is crucial for recognizing and protecting oneself from romance scams. By being aware of these tactics, individuals can better safeguard their emotions and make informed decisions when engaging in online relationships.

In conclusion, love bombing relies on emotional manipulation techniques to establish trust and control over victims. Excessive flattery, rapid relationship progression, and intense displays of affection are all strategies employed by scammers to exploit victims' desires for affection and attention. Recognizing these techniques is essential for protecting oneself from falling victim to romance scams and maintaining emotional well-being.

Building Trust and Intimacy

Scammers who engage in love bombing utilize this technique to create a false sense of intimacy and connection with their victims. They understand that building trust is essential to manipulate individuals into falling for their deceptive schemes. By employing various tactics, they aim to gain victims' reliance and establish an emotional bond that feels authentic.

One tactic used by scammers during the love bombing phase is excessive flattery. They shower their targets with compliments, making them feel special and desired. This constant praise can be intoxicating, creating a sense of euphoria and boosting victims' self-esteem. However, it is important to recognize that this flattery is part of a carefully crafted strategy meant to disarm and manipulate.

Another tactic scammers use to build trust is rapid progression in the relationship. They may declare their love early on or talk about future plans together, making victims feel like they have found their soulmate. This accelerated pace creates a false sense of intimacy and can be overwhelming for the victim. It is crucial to be cautious when faced with such rapid advancements, as genuine relationships usually require time to develop naturally.

Scammers also employ intense expressions of affection as a way to solidify the emotional connection. They may send frequent messages expressing their undying love or use romantic gestures to create a sense of security. Victims find comfort in these displays of affection, unaware that they are being manipulated into trusting someone who does not genuinely care for them.

Relying on these false feelings of comfort and security can have severe consequences. When victims become emotionally dependent on scammers, they may overlook warning signs or dismiss their gut instincts. This reliance on the scammer's affection can cloud judgment and prevent victims from seeing the truth behind the facade.

It is essential to be aware of the tactics scammers use during the love bombing phase. By understanding how they exploit emotions to establish trust and intimacy, individuals can better protect themselves from falling victim to romance scams. Remember, genuine relationships are built on mutual trust and respect that develops over time. It is important to remain cautious and verify the authenticity of any online connection before fully investing emotionally.

Conclusion

Building trust and intimacy is a critical step in the love bombing process employed by romance scammers. Through excessive flattery, rapid relationship progression, and intense expressions of affection, scammers aim to create an illusion of closeness and reliance. It is crucial for individuals to recognize these tactics and maintain a healthy level of skepticism when forming relationships online. By doing so, one can guard against falling prey to manipulative scammers seeking personal and financial gain.

Identification and explanation of common signs and behaviors associated with love bombing can help individuals recognize potential red flags and protect themselves from falling victim to a romance scam. Love bombing is a manipulative tactic used by scammers to establish trust and control over their victims. By being aware of the following signs, individuals can better distinguish between genuine affection and manipulated actions:

1. Excessive flattery: Love bombers often shower their victims with exaggerated compliments and praise in order to create an intense sense of adoration. While compliments are normal in the early stages of a relationship, an excessive amount can be a warning sign.

2. Rapid progression in the relationship: Scammers aim to accelerate the pace of the relationship in order to establish emotional intimacy quickly. They may declare their love early on, express an eagerness to commit, or talk about future plans prematurely. This can be a tactic to manipulate victims into feeling a sense of exclusivity and vulnerability.

3. Intense expressions of affection: Love bombers go above and beyond to make their victims feel cherished and desired. They may use terms of endearment excessively, send frequent messages expressing their love, or shower gifts and gestures of affection upon their victims. While these actions may seem romantic at first, they can be indicative of manipulation when combined with other signs.

It is important to note that these signs alone do not guarantee that someone is engaging in love bombing. However, if multiple signs are present in a new relationship, it is crucial to exercise caution and consider the possibility of manipulation. Trusting one's instincts and taking time to develop a genuine connection before fully investing emotionally can help mitigate the risk of falling prey to love bombing.

By being vigilant for these signs and maintaining a healthy skepticism, individuals can protect themselves from becoming victims of romance scams. It is essential to remember that genuine relationships are built on mutual trust, respect, and a gradual development of emotional intimacy. If something feels too good to be true or raises suspicions, it is important to step back, seek advice from trusted friends or family members, and take time to evaluate the situation objectively.

As individuals become more knowledgeable about the tactics employed in love bombing, they are better equipped to distinguish between genuine affection and manipulative actions. By maintaining a cautious approach and setting boundaries early on in a relationship, individuals can minimize their vulnerability to romance scams and protect their emotional well-being.

Recovery from love bombing can be a challenging and complex process. The long-term effects of love bombing on victims' self-esteem and emotional well-being can be profound, and healing from the emotional trauma requires time and support. In this section, we will discuss strategies for recovery, available resources, and guidance on rebuilding trust and developing healthy relationships after being targeted by a romance scammer.

One of the first steps in recovering from love bombing is to recognize and acknowledge the manipulation and deception that took place. It is common for victims to blame themselves or feel ashamed for falling for the scammer's tactics. However, it is important to remember that scammers are skilled manipulators who prey on vulnerabilities and use psychological techniques to gain control over their victims. Understanding this can help victims shift their focus from self-blame to self-compassion.

Seeking support from trusted friends, family members, or professionals is crucial during the recovery process. Connecting with others who have experienced similar scams can provide validation and understanding.

23

Additionally, therapists or counselors specialized in trauma and relationship issues can offer guidance and tools for healing. Support groups, both online and offline, can also provide a safe space for sharing experiences and learning from others who have gone through similar situations.

Rebuilding trust is another essential aspect of recovering from love bombing. It is natural for victims to feel hesitant or skeptical about entering new relationships after being deceived by someone they believed to be their soulmate. Taking time to heal and rebuild one's sense of self before pursuing new romantic connections can be beneficial. Engaging in self-care activities, practicing self-love, and setting boundaries are important steps in rebuilding trust in oneself.

Developing healthy relationship patterns is crucial for preventing future victimization. Learning to recognize red flags and practicing effective communication skills are essential for establishing healthier connections with others. This may involve setting clear boundaries, expressing needs and desires openly, and learning to trust one's instincts when something feels off.

It is important to note that healing from love bombing is not a linear process, and it can take time. Each individual's journey toward recovery will be unique, and it is essential to be patient with oneself throughout the process. Remembering that healing is possible and seeking support when needed can provide strength during difficult times.

There are numerous resources available for individuals who have experienced love bombing or romance scams. Online support forums, such as scam survivor groups or forums specific to romance scams, can be valuable sources of information, support, and connection with others who have had similar experiences. Many organizations also offer counseling services specifically tailored for romance scam victims, providing guidance in navigating the legal, financial, emotional, and psychological aspects of recovery.

In conclusion, recovering from love bombing requires self-compassion, support from others, and a commitment to rebuilding trust in oneself and relationships. Recognizing the manipulation that took place, seeking professional help when needed, connecting with others who have gone through similar experiences, and focusing on personal growth are vital steps in the healing process. Remember, you are not alone, and there is hope for moving forward into healthier, more fulfilling relationships.

Mirroring: Creating an Illusion of Compatibility

Mirroring is a psychological tactic commonly employed by romance scammers to create an illusion of compatibility with their victims. This technique involves the scammers carefully observing and mimicking the interests, values, and beliefs of their targets in order to establish a false sense of shared compatibility.

By mirroring their victims, scammers aim to create a deep connection and emotional bond that will make it harder for the victim to question the authenticity of the relationship. They strategically adopt the same hobbies, interests, and even political views as their targets, effectively creating an illusion of compatibility.

The purpose of mirroring is to manipulate the victim's emotions and make them believe they have found a soulmate who understands them on a profound level. By appearing to share common interests and values, scammers are able to gain the trust and affection of their victims more easily.

Victims often find themselves drawn to these scammers because they feel a strong sense of connection and validation. The mirroring technique creates the impression that the scammer truly understands and appreciates the victim, further deepening the emotional bond between them. This emotional manipulation can cloud the victim's judgment and make them more susceptible to falling for the scam.

It is important for individuals to be aware of these mirroring tactics in order to protect themselves from falling victim to romance scams. By recognizing patterns of mirroring behavior, such as sudden alignment of interests or a remarkable similarity in language and experiences, potential victims can be alerted to possible deception.

Understanding mirroring as a psychological tactic used by romance scammers is crucial in detecting and avoiding these scams. By being aware of this strategy, individuals can approach online relationships with caution and ensure that they do not become victims of emotional manipulation.

Examination of the emotional manipulation involved in mirroring:

Mirroring, as a psychological tactic used by romance scammers, has a profound impact on their victims. By mimicking the emotions of their targets, scammers create a strong bond that intensifies the victim's feelings of connection and trust. This emotional manipulation is a key element in the success of the scam.

When a scammer mirrors their victim's emotions, they provide a sense of validation and understanding. They make the victim feel seen and heard, fostering a deep sense of intimacy. By reflecting back the same emotions, desires, and vulnerabilities, scammers create an illusion of compatibility and shared experiences.

The consequences of this emotional manipulation can be devastating for victims. As the relationship progresses, the victim becomes increasingly invested, believing they have found their soulmate. They may begin to disregard any warning signs or inconsistencies because the mirroring provides a false sense of security.

However, once the scam is revealed, victims are left shattered and questioning their own judgment. They experience intense feelings of betrayal and heartbreak, realizing that the person they believed was their perfect match was merely an illusion. The impact on their perceptions of themselves and future relationships can be long-lasting.

Victims may struggle with self-doubt, blaming themselves for falling for the deception. Trust becomes a significant issue, making it difficult to form new connections or believe in genuine love again. The emotional toll experienced by victims who have been manipulated through mirroring is profound and requires time and support to heal.

It is essential for individuals to recognize the signs of mirroring in online relationships. If someone consistently reflects your emotions, interests, and experiences without any genuine differences or disagreements, it may be a red flag. Pay attention to any inconsistencies or discrepancies that may indicate a fabricated persona designed to manipulate you.

By understanding the emotional manipulation involved in mirroring, individuals can protect themselves from falling victim to romance scams. It is important to remain vigilant and trust your instincts when something feels too good to be true. Healing from the aftermath of mirroring involves rebuilding self-esteem and learning to trust again. Support networks and counseling can be invaluable resources for victims seeking to recover and move forward after such emotional manipulation.

In conclusion, mirroring is an effective psychological tactic used by romance scammers to create an illusion of compatibility with their victims. By exploiting the desire for validation and connection, scammers mirror emotions to establish trust and control. The consequences of this emotional manipulation can be devastating for victims, affecting their perceptions of themselves and future relationships. It is crucial for individuals to recognize the signs of mirroring in online relationships and seek support if they have fallen victim to this deceitful tactic.

This section of the book, "Anatomy of the Romance Scam," explores the tactic of mirroring used by romance scammers to create an illusion of compatibility with their victims. Through case studies and real-life examples, we will delve into different scenarios where scammers successfully mirrored their targets, demonstrating the effectiveness of this manipulative technique.

Case Study 1: Mary's Story
Mary, a middle-aged widow, had recently joined a dating website in hopes of finding companionship. She soon connected with a man named David, who seemed to share her interests and values. They exchanged messages daily, discussing their favorite books, hobbies, and even sharing childhood memories. As their conversations deepened, Mary felt a strong connection with David and believed she had found her soulmate.

Unbeknownst to Mary, David was a skilled scammer who meticulously crafted his online persona to mirror her interests and beliefs. He conducted thorough research on her social media profiles and used that information to create a false image of compatibility. By mirroring Mary's experiences and emotions, David successfully led her to believe they were kindred spirits.

Case Study 2: Jake's Experience

Jake, a recent divorcee, joined a popular social media platform to meet new people and potentially find love again. Within days of creating his profile, he received a message from a woman named Sarah. They quickly struck up a conversation and discovered shared interests in music, travel, and even future aspirations. Sarah seemed perfect for Jake, and he felt an instant connection.

Little did Jake know that Sarah was not who she claimed to be. Behind the attractive profile picture and engaging messages was a scammer adept at mirroring her victims. She strategically aligned herself with Jake's dreams and desires, painting herself as the ideal partner. The convincing mirroring techniques used by Sarah gave Jake a false sense of compatibility and security.

These case studies highlight how romance scammers employ mirroring as a powerful tool to deceive individuals seeking love and companionship online. By studying these examples, readers can gain a deeper understanding of the tactics employed by scammers and recognize the red flags that may indicate a potential romance scam.

It is essential to remember that these case studies represent just two examples among countless others who have fallen victim to mirroring in romance scams. By sharing these stories, our goal is to educate readers about the deceptive nature of online relationships and empower them with knowledge to protect themselves against scams.

Through awareness and vigilance, individuals can become more resilient against the manipulative tactics used by scammers. In the next section, we will explore practical advice on how to detect and recognize mirroring behavior in online relationships.

Detecting and recognizing mirroring behavior in online relationships is crucial for protecting oneself from falling victim to romance scams. By being aware of specific cues and patterns, individuals can spot potential scams and avoid being deceived by mirroring techniques.

One important cue to watch out for is similarities in language. Scammers often mirror their victims' communication style, adopting similar vocabulary, sentence structures, and even slang. They do this to create a sense of familiarity and connection with the victim. Pay attention to whether the person you're communicating with seems to use the same phrases or expressions as you. If it feels too good to be true, it might be worth investigating further.

Another key indicator of mirroring is shared experiences. Scammers will gather information about their victims through conversations and social media profiles and then use that information to create a false sense of shared history. They may claim to have had similar life experiences, hobbies, or interests as the victim. Be cautious if someone seems to have an uncanny number of overlaps with your own life. Genuine connections take time and effort to build, so be wary if it feels like someone is trying to forge an instant bond based on shared experiences.

Sudden alignment of interests is another red flag to be aware of. Scammers frequently adapt their interests and preferences to match those of their victims, hoping to appear compatible. For example, if you mention that you enjoy a particular hobby or activity, they may suddenly express the same enthusiasm for it. Take note if someone's interests seem to change abruptly or are too perfectly aligned with yours. It's important to remember that genuine compatibility is built over time and involves differences as well as similarities.

To protect yourself from falling victim to mirroring techniques, trust your instincts and remain skeptical until you have sufficient evidence of someone's authenticity. Take the time to conduct thorough research, such as reverse image searches or verifying information they provide. Use online tools and resources designed to identify scam profiles or fraudulent behavior.

Remember that mirroring is just one tactic used by romance scammers, and they will often employ a combination of techniques to deceive their victims. Stay vigilant and don't hesitate to reach out for help or advice if something feels suspicious. By being proactive and informed, you can reduce the risk of becoming another victim of the romance scam epidemic.

The long-term effects of mirroring in romance scams can be profound, leaving victims with lasting emotional turmoil and challenges in trusting others. Once victims realize they have been manipulated through mirroring tactics, they often experience feelings of betrayal and self-doubt. The realization that the connection they thought was real was actually an illusion can be devastating.

One of the primary implications of mirroring is the erosion of trust. Victims may struggle to trust their own judgment and instincts, as they question their ability to accurately assess the authenticity of a relationship. This lack of trust can extend beyond romantic relationships and affect their interactions with others in various aspects of life.

Additionally, mirroring can deeply impact victims' self-esteem. They may feel foolish or naive for falling for the scammer's false persona. The realization that someone deliberately exploited their emotions and vulnerabilities can lead to feelings of shame and self-blame. These negative emotions can have a long-lasting impact, making it challenging for victims to rebuild their self-esteem and regain confidence in themselves.

The aftermath of mirroring extends beyond individual victims and can affect their future relationships as well. After experiencing the deceptive tactics of a romance scammer, victims may find it difficult to trust potential partners. They may develop heightened skepticism and become overly cautious, which could hinder their ability to establish genuine connections with others. This fear of being manipulated again can create barriers to forming healthy relationships based on trust and authenticity.

To heal and rebuild after experiencing mirroring in a romance scam, victims need support and guidance. Seeking therapy or counseling can provide a safe space to process the emotions associated with the scam and address any underlying issues related to self-esteem or trust. Working with professionals who specialize in trauma recovery can help individuals regain a sense of self-worth and develop strategies for rebuilding their lives.

In addition to professional support, connecting with other survivors of romance scams can be beneficial. Sharing experiences with those who have gone through similar situations can provide validation, support, and a sense of community. Online forums or support groups specifically dedicated to romance scam survivors can offer valuable insights, resources, and advice for navigating the healing process.

It is essential for victims to remember that they are not at fault for being deceived by a skilled manipulator. Rebuilding self-esteem involves recognizing one's inherent worthiness and resilience. Engaging in self-care activities, setting boundaries, and practicing self-compassion are crucial steps in regaining confidence and moving forward.

Rebuilding trust in others is a gradual process. It is important to take time to reflect on past experiences, learn from them, and develop healthier patterns in forming new relationships. Learning about red flags and warning signs of romance scams can also help victims make informed decisions when engaging in online relationships in the future.

While the aftermath of mirroring in a romance scam can be challenging, with time, support, and personal growth, victims can heal and move forward toward building healthy relationships based on trust, authenticity, and mutual respect.

Gaslighting: Manipulating Reality and Emotions

Gaslighting is a manipulation tactic employed by romance scammers to control and deceive their victims. It involves the deliberate distortion of reality, leading victims to doubt their own experiences, perceptions, and sanity. Gaslighting serves a dual purpose for scammers - it allows them to maintain control over their victims and facilitates their fraudulent activities.

In the context of romance scams, gaslighting techniques may include denial, contradiction, and misdirection. Scammers use these tactics to create confusion and manipulate victims into questioning their own judgment. They may deny certain events or conversations that actually took place, contradict themselves to make victims doubt their memories, or redirect blame onto the victims themselves.

The objective of gaslighting is to undermine victims' confidence and make them reliant on the scammer's version of reality. By distorting the truth and making victims question their own sanity, scammers gain greater control over their emotions and decisions. This manipulation can be particularly devastating in romantic relationships, as victims are more likely to trust their partner and may be less vigilant to warning signs.

Gaslighting takes a toll on victims' emotional well-being. The constant questioning of reality, combined with feelings of confusion and self-doubt, can lead to increased anxiety, depression, and a sense of isolation. Victims often struggle to trust their instincts or make sound judgments in other areas of life as a result of the psychological impact.

Recognizing gaslighting in a romantic relationship is crucial for victims to protect themselves from further manipulation. Some common signs include a consistent pattern of contradictory statements from the scammer, attempts to dismiss or trivialize the victim's concerns, insistence on painting the victim as the problem, and an overall feeling of confusion or disorientation within the relationship.

Rebuilding self-esteem and recovering from gaslighting requires time and support. Victims should seek professional help from therapists or counselors who specialize in trauma and abuse recovery. Building a strong support system of friends and loved ones who can provide emotional validation and understanding is also important. Engaging in self-care activities, practicing mindfulness, and setting boundaries are essential steps towards regaining confidence and trust in oneself.

In conclusion, gaslighting is a manipulative tactic used by romance scammers to distort victims' reality and control their emotions. By recognizing the signs of gaslighting and seeking support for recovery, victims can begin to rebuild their self-esteem and regain control over their lives.

Gaslighting is a manipulative technique employed by romance scammers to control and deceive their victims. In this chapter, we will explore the specific tactics used by scammers to manipulate victims' perception of reality, creating confusion and doubt.

One common tactic employed in gaslighting is denial. Scammers may flatly deny saying or doing something, even when there is clear evidence to the contrary. By denying their actions, scammers aim to make their victims question their own memory and judgment. This can leave victims feeling disoriented and unsure of what is real.

Contradiction is another tactic commonly used in gaslighting. Scammers may say one thing and then later deny ever saying it, creating a sense of inconsistency and confusion. They may even go so far as to twist the victim's words, making them believe that they said things they never actually said. This manipulation technique further undermines a victim's confidence in their own perceptions.

Misdirection is yet another tool scammers use in gaslighting. They may distract their victims from the truth or redirect blame onto the victims themselves. By shifting focus and sowing seeds of doubt, scammers can manipulate their victims into questioning their own sanity or reliability. This can lead to feelings of insecurity and self-doubt.

It is important for individuals to recognize these gaslighting techniques in romantic relationships online. By being aware of signs such as consistent denial, contradictions, or misdirection, individuals can protect themselves from falling further into the manipulative trap set by scammers. Trusting one's instincts and seeking outside perspectives can be valuable in maintaining a clear view of reality.

Recovering from gaslighting can be a challenging process, as it often leaves victims with low self-esteem and a distorted sense of reality. It is crucial for victims to focus on rebuilding their self-esteem and regaining trust in themselves. Seeking support from friends, family, or professionals trained in counseling or trauma recovery can be instrumental in this healing journey.

There are various resources available for individuals recovering from the psychological impact of gaslighting. Support networks, therapy options, and self-help books can provide guidance and assistance for those seeking to regain their sense of self-worth and navigate through the aftermath of gaslighting.

In conclusion, gaslighting is a manipulative technique used by romance scammers to control their victims by distorting their perception of reality. Through denial, contradiction, and misdirection, scammers aim to create confusion and doubt in their victims' minds. Recognizing these tactics and seeking support are essential steps in recovering from the emotional impact of gaslighting.

The emotional toll experienced by victims of gaslighting in romance scams is profound and can have long-lasting effects on their well-being. Gaslighting is a manipulative tactic used by scammers to distort victims' perceptions of reality, leaving them feeling confused, anxious, and isolated.

One of the primary emotional impacts of gaslighting is heightened anxiety. Victims often find themselves constantly questioning their thoughts, memories, and judgments as a result of the gaslighters' manipulative tactics. They may doubt their own instincts and become overly reliant on the scammer for validation and guidance. This state of constant uncertainty can lead to heightened levels of stress and anxiety.

Depression is another common psychological effect of gaslighting in romance scams. Victims may experience a deep sense of sadness, hopelessness, and despair as they come to terms with the manipulation they have endured. The realization that they have been deceived by someone they believed to be their soulmate can be devastating and can shatter their trust in future relationships.

Feelings of isolation are also prevalent among victims of gaslighting. Scammers often isolate their victims from friends, family, and other sources of support in order to maintain control over them. Victims may feel ashamed or embarrassed about being deceived and may be hesitant to seek help or share their experiences with others. This sense of isolation can exacerbate feelings of loneliness, making it even more challenging for victims to recover from the emotional trauma inflicted upon them.

It is important for victims of gaslighting in romance scams to recognize the psychological effects they are experiencing and seek support. Therapy and counseling can be instrumental in helping victims heal from the emotional wounds inflicted by gaslighting. Support groups and online communities can also provide a safe space for victims to connect with others who have gone through similar experiences.

Rebuilding self-esteem is a crucial aspect of recovery from gaslighting. Victims may need to work on regaining trust in their own judgment, validating their feelings, and rebuilding their sense of self-worth. Through therapy, self-reflection, and support networks, victims can learn to recognize their own strengths, regain confidence, and establish healthier boundaries in future relationships.

In conclusion, the emotional impact of gaslighting in romance scams is significant and can leave victims feeling anxious, depressed, and isolated. Recognizing these emotional effects is an important step toward healing and recovery. Seeking support through therapy, counseling, and support networks can help victims rebuild their lives and regain a sense of empowerment after enduring the manipulation and deception caused by gaslighting.

Identification of common signs and behaviors that may indicate gaslighting in an online relationship:

Gaslighting is a manipulative technique commonly employed by romance scammers to control and deceive their victims. By distorting their victims' perception of reality, scammers aim to gain power and exploit vulnerabilities for personal and financial gain. It is crucial for individuals to be able to recognize the signs of gaslighting in order to protect themselves from further manipulation. Here are some common signs and behaviors that may indicate gaslighting in an online relationship:

1. Denial and Contradiction: Gaslighters often deny or contradict their victims' experiences, memories, or perceptions of events. They may dismiss valid concerns or emotions as insignificant or untrue, making the victim doubt their own judgment.

2. Constantly Changing the Narrative: Gaslighters frequently rewrite history or change the details of past conversations or interactions. They may claim that the victim misunderstood or misinterpreted what was said, causing confusion and making it difficult for the victim to trust their own memory.

3. Blaming the Victim: Gaslighters often shift blame onto their victims, making them believe that they are at fault for any issues or problems in the relationship. They may use guilt, shame, or humiliation as tools to manipulate and control the victim.

4. Minimization and Invalidating Feelings: Gaslighters downplay the significance of their victims' emotions, making them feel as though their feelings are unwarranted or exaggerated. By invalidating their experiences, gaslighters undermine the victim's sense of self-worth and confidence.

5. Isolation from Support Systems: Gaslighters often isolate their victims from friends, family, or other sources of support. They may discourage communication with others, making the victim more dependent on them for validation and emotional support.

6. Mind Games and Confusion: Gaslighters engage in mind games by intentionally creating confusion or chaos. They may give contradictory information, create inconsistencies in their stories, or manipulate the truth to keep the victim off balance and questioning their own sanity.

It is important to note that gaslighting can occur gradually over time, making it difficult for victims to recognize that they are being manipulated. However, by familiarizing oneself with these signs and behaviors, individuals can become more aware of potentially toxic dynamics within their relationships.

If you notice any of these signs in your online relationship, it is essential to trust your instincts and take steps to protect yourself. Remember that you deserve to be treated with respect and honesty. Consider reaching out to a trusted friend, family member, or professional for support and guidance as you navigate through this challenging situation.

Strategies for victims to regain confidence and trust in themselves after experiencing gaslighting:

Recovering from the psychological impact of gaslighting can be a challenging and complex process, but with time and support, it is possible to rebuild self-esteem and regain a sense of empowerment. Here are some strategies that can help victims on their journey towards healing:

1. Seek professional support: Consider reaching out to a therapist or counselor who specializes in trauma and manipulation. A professional can provide guidance, validation, and tools to help navigate the emotional aftermath of gaslighting. They can also assist in developing coping mechanisms and rebuilding self-esteem.

2. Educate yourself about gaslighting: Gain a deeper understanding of the tactics employed by gaslighters to manipulate their victims. Learning about gaslighting techniques will help you recognize them in future relationships and prevent falling into similar patterns of manipulation. By arming yourself with knowledge, you become better equipped to protect your emotional well-being.

3. Surround yourself with a support network: Connect with trusted friends, family members, or support groups who can offer empathy, validation, and solidarity. Sharing your experiences with individuals who believe and support you can provide a safe space for healing and recovery. Avoid isolating yourself, as this can perpetuate feelings of self-doubt.

4. Practice self-care: Prioritize self-care activities that promote physical, emotional, and mental well-being. Engage in activities that bring you joy, such as hobbies, exercise, or spending time in nature. Nurturing yourself helps rebuild a positive sense of self and cultivates resilience.

5. Challenge negative self-talk: Gaslighting can leave victims with deep-rooted beliefs of inadequacy and self-blame. Engage in positive affirmations and challenge negative thoughts when they arise. Remind yourself that you are deserving of love, respect, and happiness.

6. Set boundaries: Establish clear boundaries in your relationships going forward. Communicate your needs and expectations openly and assertively. Pay attention to any signs of manipulation or attempts to undermine your reality and address them promptly.

7. Take it step by step: Healing from gaslighting takes time, and everyone's journey is unique. Allow yourself the space to heal at your own pace without judgment or pressure. Remember that progress may not always be linear, and setbacks are natural.

8. Practice mindfulness: Cultivate mindfulness techniques such as meditation, deep breathing exercises, or grounding techniques. These practices can help you stay present in the moment, manage anxiety or intrusive thoughts, and foster self-compassion.

9. Focus on personal growth: Shift your energy towards personal growth and self-improvement. Explore new hobbies or interests, pursue educational opportunities, or set goals for yourself. Rebuilding your identity outside of the gaslighter's influence can be empowering and aid in the healing process.

Remember, recovering from gaslighting is a courageous act of reclaiming your power and rebuilding your life on your own terms. It may take time, but with patience, self-compassion, and support, you can emerge stronger than ever before.

Unveiling the Scammers: Profiles, Identities, and Facades

Scammers who engage in romance scams are highly skilled at creating fake profiles that appear legitimate and enticing to potential victims. In this section, we will explore the techniques these scammers employ to craft convincing facades on dating websites and social media platforms.

One of the key elements scammers include in their profiles is attractive photos. They often use stock images or steal photos from unsuspecting individuals to create an appealing visual identity. These photos are carefully selected to appeal to a wide range of people and increase the chances of attracting potential victims. Scammers may also employ photo-editing software to enhance or alter these pictures, further enhancing their attractiveness.

In addition to captivating photos, scammers include appealing personal details in their profiles. They carefully choose information that resonates with their desired targets, such as hobbies, interests, and personal achievements. By tailoring these details to align with the interests of their potential victims, scammers aim to establish a sense of shared values and compatibility.

Furthermore, scammers construct engaging narratives within their profiles. They create compelling stories about their backgrounds, careers, and life experiences to elicit empathy and build trust. These narratives are designed to captivate and draw in their targets emotionally, making them more susceptible to manipulation.

The reasons behind scammers' choices for these elements are clear - they want to attract as many potential victims as possible. By presenting themselves as desirable and relatable individuals, they increase their chances of establishing connections and ultimately deceiving unsuspecting victims.

It is important to note that these fake profiles can be difficult to spot for individuals seeking genuine connections online. Scammers go to great lengths to make their profiles appear authentic, using various tactics to deceive even the most discerning users. Therefore, it is crucial for users to be vigilant and aware of the red flags associated with romance scams.

In conclusion, scammers employ a variety of techniques when creating fake profiles for romance scams. They carefully select attractive photos, include appealing personal details, and craft engaging narratives to lure in potential victims. It is essential for individuals using dating websites and social media platforms to be cautious and skeptical when encountering profiles that seem too good to be true. By understanding the mechanics behind these fake profiles, readers can better protect themselves and their loved ones from falling victim to romance scams.

Scammers in romance scams frequently resort to stolen identities and impersonation tactics to create believable personas that deceive their targets. This section will delve into the methods scammers employ to obtain and utilize personal information, including photos, names, and even entire life stories of innocent individuals.

To begin, scammers often gather personal information from various sources, such as social media platforms, online forums, or data breaches. They meticulously research their victims, seeking details that can be used to establish credibility and trust. This information can include images, educational backgrounds, occupation details, or even hobbies and interests.

Once armed with this information, scammers skillfully construct a false identity designed to appeal to their victim's desires and preferences. They may use stolen photographs to create an attractive profile, craft compelling narratives about their lives, or forge connections based on shared interests and experiences.

It is essential to highlight the ethical and legal implications of identity theft in romance scams. When scammers steal someone's identity, they not only harm the victim by misrepresenting them but also breach their privacy and potentially tarnish their reputation. The ramifications of identity theft extend beyond the financial losses suffered by victims; they can cause long-lasting emotional distress and damage to personal relationships.

Furthermore, impersonation tactics are commonly employed by scammers to manipulate victims' emotions and establish a sense of intimacy. By assuming another person's identity, scammers exploit the trust that naturally forms in relationships and capitalize on their victim's vulnerability. The consequences of this manipulation can be devastating for the victims who invest their time, emotions, and resources into a fraudulent relationship.

Understanding the extent of identity theft in romance scams emphasizes the need for increased awareness and vigilance among individuals seeking love online. By recognizing the signs of a potential scam and being cautious with sharing personal information online, individuals can protect themselves from falling victim to these deceptive schemes.

In conclusion, stolen identities and impersonation tactics serve as critical components of romance scams. Scammers exploit personal information obtained through various means to construct believable personas that manipulate their victims emotionally. It is crucial for individuals to remain vigilant when engaging in online relationships and be wary of sharing sensitive information with strangers. By understanding the ethical and legal implications involved, we can better protect ourselves from the deceitful tactics of romance scammers.

Advanced technology plays a critical role in enabling scammers to maintain their deceptive facades and convincingly portray themselves as genuine individuals. This section will delve into the various technological tools and resources that scammers employ to perpetuate their scams.

One of the methods scammers utilize is photo-editing software, which allows them to manipulate images to create attractive and appealing profiles. They can enhance their physical appearance or even use someone else's photos altogether. By presenting themselves as physically attractive, scammers aim to capture the attention and interest of potential victims. This manipulation of visual imagery serves to establish a false sense of trust and allure.

In addition to photo editing, scammers also employ voice-changing technology. During phone calls or voice messages, scammers may alter their voices to sound different from their true identities. This tactic adds another layer of deception, making it more difficult for victims to suspect any wrongdoing. By modifying their voices, scammers can further manipulate emotions and establish a connection based on false premises.

Perhaps one of the most concerning advancements in technology used by scammers is deepfake technology. Deepfakes involve the use of artificial intelligence algorithms to superimpose one person's face onto another person's body or create entirely fabricated videos. Scammers may use deepfake technology to simulate video chats with unsuspecting victims, portraying themselves as real and present in the conversation. This sophisticated technology allows scammers to deceive victims on a whole new level, blurring the lines between reality and fiction.

By utilizing these advanced technologies, scammers elevate their manipulation tactics to an unprecedented level of sophistication. They exploit the vulnerabilities of online communication platforms to create a convincing facade that can easily deceive even the most cautious individuals. The use of photo-editing software, voice-changing technology, and deepfake technology demonstrates the lengths scammers are willing to go to maintain their deceitful personas.

It's essential for individuals to be aware of these technological advancements employed by scammers. Recognizing that such tools exist can help potential victims approach online relationships with caution and skepticism. Understanding that scammers can leverage these technologies helps empower individuals to critically evaluate any suspicious behaviors or inconsistencies they may encounter online.

As society continues to evolve and embrace new technologies, it's crucial for online platforms, such as dating websites and social media platforms, to stay vigilant and adapt their security measures accordingly. Preventative measures should be implemented to detect and prevent the use of manipulative technologies by scammers. User safety should be a top priority, and platforms must take responsibility for ensuring the integrity of their user base.

In conclusion, advanced technology plays a significant role in allowing scammers to maintain their deceptive facades. Photo-editing software, voice-changing technology, and deepfake technology are among the tools scammers use to convincingly portray themselves as genuine individuals. It is important for individuals to be aware of these advancements and approach online relationships with caution. Online platforms must also take responsibility for implementing effective security measures to protect their users from falling victim to these sophisticated scams.

Scammers are cunning in their efforts to avoid detection and law enforcement. They employ various tactics to ensure they remain under the radar and continue their fraudulent activities unchecked. In this section, we will explore the measures scammers take to evade detection and the challenges faced by authorities in tracking them down and prosecuting them.

One of the primary ways scammers evade detection is by using virtual private networks (VPNs) to hide their IP addresses. By masking their true location, scammers can make it difficult for law enforcement agencies to trace their online activities back to them. VPNs allow scammers to appear as if they are accessing the internet from a different country or region, further complicating the investigation process.

Additionally, scammers often operate from countries with lax cybercrime laws. By choosing jurisdictions that provide minimal legal consequences for their actions, scammers can carry out their fraudulent activities with relative impunity. These countries may lack the resources or willingness to cooperate with international law enforcement efforts, making it challenging to apprehend and prosecute scammers operating within their borders.

The international nature of romance scams poses another significant challenge for law enforcement agencies. Scammers exploit the borderless nature of the internet to target victims from all around the world while operating from different locations themselves. This makes coordination between law enforcement agencies in different countries vital for effective investigations, but it also adds complexity to the process. The lack of standardized laws and protocols across jurisdictions further compounds these challenges.

Furthermore, scammers continually adapt and evolve their tactics to stay ahead of law enforcement efforts. As authorities become aware of specific techniques used by scammers, such as new software or communication platforms, scammers quickly adapt their methods to avoid detection. This cat-and-mouse game between scammers and law enforcement agencies requires constant vigilance and ongoing efforts to stay updated on the latest trends in romance scams.

Despite these challenges, there have been notable successes in arresting and prosecuting romance scammers. International collaborations between law enforcement agencies have led to significant arrests and dismantling of scamming networks. However, due to the sheer scale of the issue and the ever-changing nature of scams, eradicating romance scams entirely remains a persistent challenge.

In conclusion, romance scammers employ various strategies to evade detection and law enforcement. Their use of VPNs, operating from countries with lax cybercrime laws, and constantly adapting their tactics present formidable challenges for authorities seeking to bring these criminals to justice. Addressing these challenges requires international collaboration, improved legal frameworks, and ongoing efforts to stay updated on emerging trends in romance scams.

Dating websites and social media platforms play a significant role in the prevalence of romance scams. These platforms provide scammers with easy access to a large pool of potential victims, making it essential for them to take responsibility for preventing and addressing these scams.

An analysis of the vulnerabilities within dating websites and social media platforms reveals the ways in which scammers are able to operate unchecked. For instance, scammers can create multiple fake profiles using different email addresses and IP addresses, allowing them to target numerous victims simultaneously. The lack of stringent verification processes on these platforms makes it easier for scammers to create convincing personas and gain the trust of unsuspecting individuals.

To enhance user safety and prevent romance scams, dating websites and social media platforms should implement several measures. Firstly, they should strengthen their user authentication processes by implementing more robust identity verification measures. This could include requesting additional personal information or implementing facial recognition technology to confirm users' identities.

Secondly, these platforms need to invest in advanced fraud detection systems. By utilizing machine learning algorithms and artificial intelligence, they can identify suspicious patterns of behavior indicative of a scammer. This includes monitoring for accounts that exhibit characteristics such as sending large numbers of unsolicited messages, requesting money, or displaying inconsistent information in their profiles.

Furthermore, improved user education and awareness campaigns are crucial for preventing romance scams. Dating websites and social media platforms should provide clear guidelines and resources on how to identify and report suspected scammers. They can also actively promote educational content about common red flags and warning signs associated with romance scams.

Additionally, it is imperative for online platforms to take swift action upon receiving reports of suspected scams. This involves investigating reported profiles promptly and removing those that are found to be fraudulent. Timely responses demonstrate a commitment to user safety and discourage scammers from continuing their deceptive activities.

By actively engaging in efforts to prevent romance scams, dating websites and social media platforms can help protect their users from falling victim to these deceitful schemes. It is essential that they prioritize the security and protection of their users and work collaboratively with law enforcement agencies to detect, investigate, and prosecute cybercriminals involved in romance scams.

In conclusion, dating websites and social media platforms have a significant role to play in combatting romance scams. By addressing the vulnerabilities within their platforms, implementing robust user authentication processes, investing in fraud detection systems, providing user education, and taking swift action on reported profiles, these platforms can contribute to reducing the prevalence of romance scams. It is crucial for them to recognize their responsibility in ensuring the security and protection of their users.

The Mechanics of Online Connections: Dating Websites and Social Media Platforms

Online dating websites and social media platforms have become popular avenues for individuals seeking romance and companionship. However, these platforms also present opportunities for scammers to exploit vulnerable individuals for personal and financial gain.

Dating websites, such as Match.com, eHarmony, and Plenty of Fish, offer users the ability to create profiles and connect with potential partners based on shared interests and preferences. These platforms have experienced significant growth in recent years, with millions of users worldwide. Similarly, social media platforms like Facebook, Instagram, and Twitter allow individuals to connect with others and establish relationships online.

The rise in popularity of these platforms has unfortunately led to an increase in romance scams. Scammers are adept at creating fake profiles that appear legitimate and genuine, often using stolen photos and personal information. They employ various tactics to initiate contact with potential victims and build trust over time.

Dating websites and social media platforms provide scammers with a wide pool of potential victims who are eager to find love and companionship. This creates an environment where scammers can easily prey on vulnerable individuals who may be emotionally invested in the idea of a romantic relationship.

It is important to understand the vulnerabilities within these platforms that scammers exploit. Inadequate security measures, lack of identity verification, and the ease with which scammers can create fake profiles all contribute to the success of romance scams. Additionally, the anonymity provided by these platforms allows scammers to hide their true identities and motives.

By familiarizing yourself with the inner workings of dating websites and social media platforms, you can better protect yourself from falling victim to a romance scam. Recognizing the potential for exploitation and understanding the tactics employed by scammers is crucial in maintaining your safety online.

In the following sections, we will delve deeper into the specific vulnerabilities within these platforms and explore real-life examples of romance scams that originated from dating websites and social media platforms. We will also discuss the responsibility of these platforms in preventing and addressing romance scams. Finally, we will provide practical advice and strategies for protecting yourself from becoming a victim of a romance scam while using online platforms.

Vulnerabilities within dating websites and social media platforms are a key factor in the success of romance scams. These platforms provide scammers with an opportunity to exploit unsuspecting individuals due to various weaknesses and shortcomings.

One vulnerability lies in the inadequate security measures implemented by some dating websites and social media platforms. These platforms may not have robust systems in place to detect and remove fraudulent accounts or to monitor suspicious activities. Scammers can easily create fake profiles and use them to deceive and manipulate their victims. Without proper security measures, it becomes easier for scammers to hide their true identities and intentions.

Another vulnerability is the lack of identity verification on many platforms. While some dating websites and social media platforms have implemented verification processes, they are often not foolproof. Scammers can exploit this weakness by using stolen identities or creating false documents to pass through the verification process undetected. This allows them to establish trust with their victims and appear legitimate.

Additionally, the ease with which scammers can create fake profiles is a major vulnerability within these platforms. They can easily upload stolen photos or use stock images to create attractive profiles that lure in unsuspecting individuals. Furthermore, scammers can quickly modify their profiles and adapt their personas to suit their victims' desires and interests. This level of adaptability makes it difficult for users to distinguish between genuine individuals and fraudsters.

It is crucial for users of dating websites and social media platforms to be aware of these vulnerabilities and take steps to protect themselves. This includes being cautious when interacting with individuals online, verifying identities through independent means, and reporting suspicious or fraudulent behavior to platform administrators. By understanding the vulnerabilities within these platforms, users can become more vigilant and reduce their risk of falling victim to romance scams.

In conclusion, dating websites and social media platforms have vulnerabilities that scammers exploit to carry out romance scams. These vulnerabilities include inadequate security measures, a lack of identity verification, and the ease with which scammers can create fake profiles. It is essential for users to be aware of these weaknesses and take proactive measures to protect themselves from falling victim to deception and manipulation online.

Case studies play a crucial role in understanding the mechanics of romance scams that originate from dating websites and social media platforms. By analyzing real-life examples, we can gain valuable insights into how scammers initiate contact, build relationships, and manipulate their victims through these online avenues.

In one case study, we explore the story of Sarah, a middle-aged woman who joined a popular dating website in search of companionship. She soon received a message from a charming man who claimed to be a successful businessman from another country. Their conversations quickly progressed from casual chats to declarations of love and promises of a future together.

The scammer utilized the dating website's messaging system to establish trust and emotional connection with Sarah. He showered her with affectionate messages and compliments, making her feel special and desired. Over time, he revealed personal details about his life and shared intimate stories, further deepening the emotional bond between them.

As the relationship progressed, the scammer began requesting financial assistance from Sarah, citing various emergencies and business setbacks. Under the guise of needing funds to overcome these challenges, he convinced her to send money through wire transfers or gift cards. Sarah, believing she was helping her beloved partner, complied without realizing she was being deceived.

Another case study involves John, a divorcee who connected with a woman through a social media platform. They started chatting on the platform's messaging feature, sharing their interests, dreams, and aspirations. The scammer portrayed herself as an attractive and successful individual, using stolen photographs and false information to create an appealing persona.

As their online relationship developed, the scammer gradually introduced stories of financial hardships and asked John for monetary assistance. Believing he had found genuine love, John willingly sent money to support his partner's supposed financial struggles. Sadly, it was only later that he discovered the truth – he had fallen victim to an elaborate romance scam.

These case studies demonstrate how scammers exploit the anonymity and perceived trustworthiness of dating websites and social media platforms to manipulate their victims emotionally and financially. By establishing romantic connections and gaining their victims' trust over time, scammers can successfully deceive individuals into providing them with money or personal information.

It is essential for users of these platforms to remain vigilant and cautious when engaging in online relationships. By recognizing the warning signs discussed in this book and learning from these real-life examples, individuals can protect themselves from falling victim to romance scams.

In conclusion, case studies provide valuable insights into the mechanics of romance scams originating from dating websites and social media platforms. They highlight the tactics used by scammers to exploit emotions and deceive unsuspecting individuals. By studying these real-life examples, readers can better understand the techniques employed by scammers and take proactive measures to protect themselves online.

Dating websites and social media platforms have become popular avenues for individuals seeking romance and connections. Unfortunately, they have also become breeding grounds for romance scams. These platforms play a significant role in facilitating the initial contact between scammers and their victims, making it crucial to discuss the responsibility of these platforms in preventing and addressing romance scams.

Dating websites and social media platforms must recognize their role in providing a safe environment for users. They should prioritize implementing robust security measures to detect and remove fraudulent accounts. This includes verifying user identities through stringent authentication processes and employing advanced technology to identify suspicious activities.

To effectively combat romance scams, it is essential for these platforms to cooperate with law enforcement agencies. By collaborating with authorities, they can aid in the investigation and prosecution of scammers, ultimately deterring future fraudulent activities. This collaboration may involve sharing information about suspicious accounts, assisting in tracing financial transactions, and providing support during legal proceedings.

Furthermore, dating websites and social media platforms should actively educate their users about the risks associated with online relationships and provide guidelines on how to identify and report potential scams. It is their responsibility to inform users about red flags to watch out for, such as requests for money or personal information early on in a relationship. By offering educational resources and fostering awareness, these platforms can empower their users to protect themselves from falling victim to romance scams.

While some dating websites and social media platforms have taken steps to address romance scams, there is still room for improvement. Platforms should allocate sufficient resources to develop and maintain effective scam detection algorithms that can identify suspicious behavior patterns and flag potentially fraudulent accounts. Additionally, they should invest in user support services that offer assistance to victims who have been deceived by scammers on their platform.

Ultimately, the responsibility of dating websites and social media platforms goes beyond merely providing an avenue for connection. They must actively work towards creating a secure environment where users can engage in genuine relationships without fear of falling victim to deception. Only through a collective effort between the platforms, law enforcement agencies, and users themselves can we hope to mitigate the prevalence of romance scams in online spaces.

Prevention strategies are crucial in protecting oneself from falling victim to a romance scam. Whether using dating websites or social media platforms, there are practical steps that users can take to safeguard their personal and financial well-being.

1. Verify identities: Be cautious when connecting with new individuals online. Take the time to verify their identities by conducting a reverse image search or searching for their social media profiles. Look for inconsistencies or red flags that may indicate a fake profile.

2. Maintain privacy: Be mindful of the information you share online, especially with individuals you have recently connected with. Avoid sharing personal details such as your full name, address, or financial information until you have established a genuine and trustworthy relationship.

3. Recognize suspicious behavior: Pay attention to any signs of suspicious behavior or requests for money or personal information. Romance scammers often use sob stories or emergencies to manipulate victims into providing financial assistance. Trust your instincts and be wary of anyone who seems too good to be true.

4. Communicate outside the platform: Once you have established a connection with someone online, consider moving communication to another platform or channel. Scammers may try to keep interactions solely within the dating website or social media platform to avoid detection. By communicating through alternative means, such as email or phone calls, you can further verify the person's identity.

5. Conduct background checks: If you feel uncertain about someone you've met online, consider conducting a background check. Various online services provide access to public records and can help confirm someone's identity and background information.

6. Educate yourself: Stay informed about the latest scams and tactics used by romance scammers. Familiarize yourself with common red flags and warning signs, such as excessive flattery, inconsistent stories, or pressure for quick financial assistance. By staying educated, you can better protect yourself from falling victim to these deceptive schemes.

Remember, prevention is key when it comes to romance scams. By implementing these practical strategies and remaining vigilant, you can significantly reduce your risk of becoming a victim. Online platforms must also take responsibility by implementing stronger security measures, identity verification processes, and actively removing fraudulent accounts to create safer environments for their users.

Red Flags and Warning Signs: How to Spot a Romance Scam

In the world of online relationships, it is crucial to remain vigilant and aware of potential red flags and warning signs that may indicate a romance scam. By recognizing these indicators early on, you can protect yourself from falling victim to heartless deception. Here are some common red flags to watch out for:

1. Suspiciously quick progression: One of the telltale signs of a romance scam is when the relationship progresses at an unnaturally fast pace. Scammers often try to establish a sense of trust and intimacy within a short period, making extravagant promises or declarations of love too soon. Remember, genuine relationships take time to develop.

2. Poor grammar and inconsistency: Pay attention to the quality of communication in your online relationship. Scammers may display poor grammar, inconsistent writing styles, or use generic responses that may seem impersonal. These signs can indicate that the person you're interacting with is not who they claim to be.

3. Unusual behavior and requests: Be wary of any behavior that seems unusual or raises doubts about the authenticity of the relationship. Scammers may employ tactics such as excessive flattery, overly personal questions, or requests for financial assistance, gifts, or personal information. If someone you've just met online is asking for money or pressuring you into providing personal details, it's likely a red flag.

To protect yourself from falling victim to a romance scam, consider the following strategies:

1. Conduct thorough research: Take the time to verify the identity of your potential partner. Perform reverse image searches on their profile pictures to ensure they are not taken from other sources. Look for inconsistencies in their stories or information provided.

2. Keep communication within the dating platform or social media site: Until you feel comfortable enough to move communication elsewhere, it is wise to keep conversations restricted to the platform where you initially

connected. This provides an additional layer of security and allows you to report any suspicious activity if needed.

3. Trust your intuition: Always listen to your gut instincts. If something feels off about a person or situation, don't ignore those feelings. Your intuition can often pick up on subtle cues that something is not right. It's better to err on the side of caution and protect yourself.

Remember, spotting red flags and warning signs is essential in preventing yourself from becoming a victim of a romance scam. By staying aware and educated, you can navigate the online dating world more safely and protect yourself from heartbreak and financial loss.

If you suspect that you have encountered a romance scam, it is crucial to report it immediately to local law enforcement agencies or cybercrime units dedicated to handling these types of cases. There are also trustworthy organizations available that specialize in assisting romance scam victims, providing emotional support, and offering guidance on legal matters.

By staying informed and empowered, we can collectively combat the menace of romance scams and create a safer online environment for all individuals seeking love and companionship.

Guide readers on recognizing suspicious behavior, inconsistencies, and requests for money or personal information.

Remaining vigilant and questioning any behavior that seems too good to be true or raises doubts about the authenticity of the relationship is crucial when it comes to spotting a romance scam. Scammers often employ tactics aimed at gaining trust quickly, so it's essential to stay alert.

One red flag to watch out for is poor grammar and inconsistency in communication. If you notice frequent grammatical errors, inconsistent writing styles, or repeated use of generic responses, it could indicate that the person you're talking to is not who they claim to be. Scammers may use automated scripts or have difficulty maintaining a consistent persona, so be wary of these signs.

Another warning sign is unusual behavior and requests. Excessive flattery, overly personal questions early on, or sudden requests for financial assistance, gifts, or personal information should raise suspicion. Remember that genuine relationships take time to develop, and anyone pressuring you for money or personal details should be treated with caution.

To protect yourself from falling victim to a romance scam, it's important to establish trust gradually. Conduct thorough research on potential partners, including reverse image searches to ensure their profile pictures are not stolen from other sources. Keep conversations within the dating platform or social media site until you feel comfortable enough to move communication elsewhere. Sharing personal or financial information should only be done once trust has been thoroughly established.

It's also essential to listen to your intuition and trust your gut instincts. If something feels off or too good to be true, it's better to err on the side of caution. Don't ignore your inner voice if it raises concerns about a person or situation.

Recognizing warning signs goes beyond just spotting suspicious behavior. Scammers often avoid video calls or provide excuses for not being able to meet in person. They may try to isolate you from friends and family by discouraging contact with them or making false claims about their intentions. Be aware of these tactics as they are commonly employed by scammers.

If you suspect that you may be involved in a romance scam, it is important to report it. Contact your local law enforcement agency or cybercrime unit to report the suspected scam. There are also organizations that specialize in assisting romance scam victims, providing emotional support and guidance on legal matters. Seek advice from professionals who can help you recover emotionally and financially from the impact of a romance scam.

Remember, recognizing red flags and warning signs is a crucial step in protecting yourself from falling victim to a romance scam. Stay vigilant, trust your instincts, and seek help if you suspect you may be involved in a fraudulent relationship.

In order to protect oneself from falling victim to a romance scam, there are several strategies that individuals can employ. These strategies aim to empower readers to make informed decisions when engaging with potential romantic partners online.

Firstly, it is essential to conduct thorough research on potential partners. This includes performing reverse image searches to ensure that the photographs being used are not stolen from other sources. Scammers often use fake profiles with attractive pictures to establish trust and manipulate their victims. By conducting these checks, individuals can identify any inconsistencies or signs of deception.

Additionally, it is prudent to keep conversations within the dating platform or social media site until a sufficient level of comfort and trust has been established. Using these platforms allows for greater safety and accountability as there is a record of all communication. It also provides an opportunity for the platform's security measures to identify and flag potential scammers.

Lastly, it is crucial to listen to one's intuition and trust their gut instincts. If something feels off or too good to be true about a person or situation, it is essential to take a step back and reassess the situation. Scammers often use manipulation tactics to exploit vulnerabilities and gain control over their victims. By trusting one's instincts, individuals can avoid falling prey to these deceitful schemes.

By following these strategies, readers can significantly reduce their risk of becoming victims of romance scams. It is important to remain vigilant, stay informed about the warning signs, and remember that personal safety should always be a top priority in the online dating world.

In addition to the common red flags and warning signs discussed earlier in this book, there are other indicators that may suggest you are dealing with a romance scam. One such sign is when the person you are communicating with avoids video calls or makes excuses for not being able to meet in person. Scammers often use images stolen from the internet or from other individuals, and they may be hesitant to engage in video calls because it can reveal their true identity.

Real-life stories from victims who ignored these warning signs provide a stark reminder of the severe consequences that can result from falling for a romance scam. These stories serve as cautionary tales, highlighting the importance of paying attention to any suspicious behavior or inconsistencies in an online relationship.

Scammers will often employ tactics aimed at isolating their victims from their friends and family. By cutting off external influences that may raise suspicions, scammers are able to maintain control over their victims. This isolation can make it even more difficult for victims to recognize the signs of a scam and seek help. It is crucial to remain connected with trusted loved ones and maintain open lines of communication to ensure you have a support system in place.

Recognizing these additional warning signs and understanding the tactics scammers use can help you protect yourself from becoming a victim of a romance scam. By staying vigilant, conducting thorough research on potential partners, and trusting your instincts, you can minimize the risk of falling prey to these deceitful schemes.

If you suspect that you may be involved in a romance scam or have encountered suspicious behavior online, it is important to report it to local law enforcement agencies or cybercrime units. There are also numerous organizations that specialize in assisting romance scam victims, providing emotional support, guidance on legal matters, and resources for recovery. Seeking advice from professionals who can help you navigate the aftermath of a romance scam is essential for your emotional and financial well-being.

Remember, knowledge is power when it comes to protecting yourself from romance scams. Stay informed, trust your instincts, and reach out for assistance if you encounter any warning signs or suspect fraudulent activity.

Resources and guidance for reporting suspected scams and seeking help:

If you suspect that you may be the target of a romance scam, it is crucial to take immediate action to protect yourself and seek assistance. Here are some valuable resources and guidance to help you navigate through this challenging situation:

1. Contact Local Law Enforcement Agencies or Cybercrime Units:
Reporting the suspected scam to your local law enforcement agencies or cybercrime units is an essential step in holding scammers accountable and preventing them from victimizing others. These agencies have specialized units dedicated to handling cybercrimes, including romance scams. They can guide you on how to proceed with your case and provide additional support.

2. Seek Assistance from Trustworthy Organizations:
There are numerous organizations that specialize in assisting romance scam victims, providing emotional support, and offering guidance on legal matters. These organizations understand the unique challenges faced by victims and can provide valuable resources. Some notable organizations include:

- Romance Scams Now: A nonprofit organization that offers support, education, and advocacy for romance scam victims. They have a comprehensive website with helpful articles, resources, and a live chat feature for immediate assistance.
- Cybercrime Support Network: A national organization that connects victims of cybercrime with resources, support services, and local law enforcement agencies.
- Better Business Bureau (BBB) Scam Tracker: The BBB provides a Scam Tracker tool where individuals can report scams, search for reported scams in their area, and receive tips on how to avoid falling victim to various types of fraud.

3. Consult with Professionals:

Seeking advice from professionals who specialize in helping romance scam victims can be immensely beneficial for recovery, both emotionally and financially. Consider reaching out to the following professionals:

- Therapists or Counselors: A therapist or counselor experienced in trauma recovery can provide vital emotional support and guidance as you navigate the aftermath of the scam.
- Legal Professionals: If the scam has resulted in significant financial loss or other legal implications, consulting with an attorney who specializes in cybercrimes or fraud can help you understand your rights and explore possible legal actions.
- Financial Advisors: If your finances have been compromised by the scam, consider consulting a financial advisor who can assist you in managing debts, rebuilding credit, and developing a plan for recovering financially.

Remember, reaching out for help is not a sign of weakness; it's a proactive step towards reclaiming your life. By leveraging these resources and seeking professional assistance, you can begin the healing process and regain control over your future.

Conclusion:
Recognizing red flags and warning signs is crucial in protecting yourself from falling victim to a romance scam. However, if you do find yourself ensnared in one, don't hesitate to reach out for help. Reporting the scam to local law enforcement agencies or cybercrime units can help prevent further harm, while organizations specializing in assisting romance scam victims can provide valuable support and guidance. Additionally, consulting professionals such as therapists, legal experts, and financial advisors can aid in your recovery journey. Remember, there are resources available to help you through this difficult time – you don't have to face it alone.

Real-Life Stories: Tales of Deception and Betrayal

Introduction to Real-Life Stories:

In this chapter, we delve into the personal accounts of survivors who have experienced the devastating impact of romance scams. These stories are not only eye-opening but also serve as crucial tools for understanding the tactics employed by scammers and gaining valuable insights into their deceptive practices. By listening to these real-life tales of deception and betrayal, we can learn from the experiences of others and better protect ourselves from falling victim to these insidious crimes.

Why are these stories important? They provide firsthand perspectives on the emotional journey that victims go through, from the initial excitement of finding love online to the heart-wrenching realization that it was all a lie. Hearing these stories helps us comprehend the psychological trauma inflicted by scammers who exploit their victims' trust and emotions.

By sharing stories from different demographics, backgrounds, and experiences, we aim to present a comprehensive understanding of the impact of romance scams. Each survivor's account offers unique insights into the tactics employed by scammers, helping us recognize the warning signs and red flags that indicate a potential scam.

Throughout this chapter, you will read accounts from individuals who have been targeted by romance scammers, each with their own story to tell. By immersing ourselves in these narratives, we gain a deeper understanding of the emotional manipulation and deceit used by perpetrators. We hope that these stories empower readers to protect themselves and their loved ones from becoming victims and to navigate their way through the aftermath if they have already been affected.

Strap in as we embark on this emotional journey of deception and betrayal, and prepare to hear firsthand accounts that shed light on the intricate workings of the romance scam. These stories serve as reminders that awareness, resilience, and education are essential in combating this heartbreaking cybercrime.

67

Personal Accounts from Survivors:

- Lisa's Story: A Middle-Aged Widow's Quest for Love

Lisa, a middle-aged widow, shares her story of falling victim to a romance scam after seeking companionship on a dating website. She recounts the initial excitement of meeting someone who seemed perfect for her, only to discover that he was a scammer manipulating her emotions and exploiting her vulnerabilities. Lisa discusses the financial loss she experienced and the emotional toll it took on her self-esteem and trust in others.

- David's Experience: A Military Veteran's Online Deception

David, a military veteran, recounts his encounter with a scammer posing as a fellow veteran on a social media platform. He candidly reveals the emotional manipulation he experienced, including the scammer using his military background to establish trust and manipulate his feelings of loyalty. David shares the devastating impact the scam had on his financial stability and mental well-being.

- Fatima's Journey: A Young Professional's Hope Shattered

Fatima, a young professional searching for love online, narrates her experience of falling prey to a romance scam. She discusses how the scammer exploited her desire for connection and deceived her into sending money under false pretenses. Fatima opens up about the emotional trauma she endured and the long-lasting effects it had on her self-confidence and ability to trust others.

- Mark's Lesson: A Widower's Second Chance at Love Gone Wrong

Mark, a widower looking for love again, shares his heartbreaking story of being targeted by a romance scammer. He discusses how the scammer used

69

emotional manipulation tactics to gain his trust and exploit his vulnerability after losing his spouse. Mark reflects on the financial hardships he faced as a result and the profound impact it had on his ability to open himself up to new relationships.

These personal accounts offer a glimpse into the diverse experiences of individuals who have fallen victim to romance scams. By sharing stories from different demographics and backgrounds, readers can develop a comprehensive understanding of the devastating impact these scams have on victims' lives. These real-life narratives serve as cautionary tales, highlighting the tactics employed by scammers and emphasizing the importance of awareness and vigilance when seeking love online.

Through these personal accounts, readers are encouraged to reflect on their own experiences and consider how they can protect themselves and their loved ones from becoming victims. The stories also provide validation and support for those who have survived romance scams, letting them know they are not alone in their struggles.

Emotional Journey and Impact:

The emotional journey that victims of romance scams go through is both tumultuous and devastating. It begins with a sense of excitement and hope as they believe they have found their soulmate or the love they have been searching for. The initial stages of the scam are filled with flattery, affectionate messages, and promises of a future together. Victims become emotionally invested, believing that they have finally found someone who truly understands and cares for them.

However, as the scam progresses, the truth slowly starts to unravel. Victims often experience a rollercoaster of emotions as they begin to suspect that something is not right. They may feel confused, conflicted, and even guilty for doubting their partner. This internal struggle is intensified by the manipulation tactics employed by scammers, such as gaslighting, which makes victims doubt their own intuition and reality.

When victims finally discover the deception, it is a devastating blow to their emotional well-being. They may experience a profound sense of betrayal and heartbreak as they come to terms with the fact that the person they believed to be their soulmate was merely a fraud. Trust, which is crucial in any relationship, is shattered, leaving victims feeling vulnerable and wary of forming new connections.

The psychological trauma caused by romance scams can be long-lasting. Victims may suffer from anxiety, depression, post-traumatic stress disorder (PTSD), or other mental health issues. The emotional impact can also extend to other areas of their lives, affecting their self-esteem, self-worth, and ability to trust others. Many victims feel a deep sense of shame and embarrassment for having been deceived, further complicating their healing process.

It is important to recognize and acknowledge the emotional toll that romance scams take on their victims. By understanding the depth of these emotions, we can better support survivors and provide them with the compassion and resources they need to heal. Recovery from a romance scam is a complex and individual process, but with time, therapy, and a strong support system, victims can regain control of their lives and restore their emotional well-being.

In conclusion, the emotional journey experienced by victims of romance scams is characterized by excitement, hope, confusion, betrayal, and heartbreak. The psychological impact can be severe and long-lasting, affecting victims' mental health, self-esteem, and ability to trust again. Recognizing and addressing these emotional challenges is essential for survivors to move forward on their journey towards healing and rebuilding their lives.

Identifying commonalities among the shared stories, we can gain valuable insights into the tactics employed by romance scammers. These scammers are skilled at exploiting victims' emotions and manipulating their desires for love and companionship. By understanding these tactics, we can better protect ourselves and others from falling victim to these deceitful schemes.

One recurring tactic used by scammers is the creation of a false sense of intimacy and connection. They often employ love bombing techniques, showering their victims with affectionate messages, compliments, and promises of a future together. By bombarding their targets with attention and flattery, scammers quickly establish trust and create a strong emotional bond.

Another tactic commonly deployed by scammers is the use of sob stories and fabricated hardships. They prey on their victims' empathy and compassion, sharing stories of financial struggles, family emergencies, or medical conditions to elicit sympathy. This manipulation tactic plays on the victims' desire to help and be there for someone they care about.

Scammers are also known to exploit their victims' vulnerabilities and insecurities. They identify individuals who may be feeling lonely, isolated, or longing for companionship, and use this knowledge to their advantage. They offer a listening ear, claiming to understand their victims' deepest desires and fears. This emotional connection makes it easier for scammers to manipulate victims into sending money or divulging personal information.

Additionally, scammers often employ mirroring techniques. They carefully study their victims' online profiles, social media posts, and conversations to mirror their interests, values, and beliefs. By presenting themselves as ideal matches, scammers create the illusion of compatibility and reinforce the emotional connection they have established.

Gaslighting is another tactic utilized by scammers to deceive their victims. They manipulate reality and emotions by distorting facts, denying previous statements or actions, and making their targets doubt their own experiences. This psychological manipulation undermines victims' confidence and causes them to question their own judgment.

By analyzing these tactics used by romance scammers in real-life stories, we can identify warning signs to look out for. It is important to maintain a healthy level of skepticism when engaging in online relationships and to be cautious of individuals who exhibit these manipulative behaviors. Trust should be earned gradually over time rather than given freely based solely on virtual interactions.

Remember that scammers often rely on urgency and pressure to make their victims act quickly without thinking rationally. Take the time to verify information, ask questions, and conduct thorough research if something seems suspicious. It is crucial to prioritize personal safety and protect oneself from potential harm.

In conclusion, analyzing the common tactics employed by romance scammers can provide valuable insights into the deception and manipulation they employ. By being aware of these tactics, individuals can better protect themselves and their loved ones from falling victim to romance scams.

Insights for Prevention and Empowerment:

As we delve into the real-life stories of individuals who have fallen victim to romance scams, it is crucial to extract valuable lessons and insights that can help readers recognize warning signs and protect themselves from similar deceptions. By understanding the tactics employed by scammers, we can empower ourselves with knowledge to avoid becoming victims of this devastating cybercrime.

One recurring theme in these stories is the initial excitement and emotional connection that victims felt when they first encountered the scammer. It is important to acknowledge that scammers are skilled manipulators who know how to exploit our desires for love, companionship, and validation. By being aware of our vulnerabilities, we can approach online relationships with caution and skepticism.

One key lesson learned from survivors is the importance of maintaining a healthy level of skepticism when engaging with someone online. Scammers will often try to rush the relationship, proclaiming love and commitment at an alarming pace. They may shower their victims with compliments and affection, using love bombing techniques to establish trust and control. By recognizing this tactic, we can take a step back and evaluate the authenticity of the relationship before getting too emotionally invested.

Another insight gained from survivors' stories is the significance of paying attention to inconsistencies and red flags. Scammers may use fake profiles or stolen identities, making it essential to be vigilant in verifying their information. Look out for discrepancies in their stories, conflicting details, or requests for money or personal information early on in the relationship. Trust your instincts and don't hesitate to ask questions or do some research to confirm their claims.

Empowering messages of resilience, recovery, and encouragement also emerge from these survivors' accounts. It is crucial to remember that falling victim to a romance scam does not define one's worth or intelligence. Scammers prey on vulnerability and manipulate emotions, making anyone susceptible to their deceitful tactics. By seeking support from loved ones, considering professional counseling if needed, and utilizing available resources for recovery, survivors can regain their sense of self-worth and move forward with their lives.

In conclusion, these real-life stories serve as powerful reminders of the importance of awareness and vigilance when navigating the online dating world. By learning from the experiences of others, we can recognize warning signs, protect ourselves from falling victim to deception, and ultimately reclaim our power. It is through education, prevention efforts, and supporting one another that we can combat the romance scam epidemic and create a safer digital landscape for all.

Consequences: Emotional, Financial, and Psychological Fallout

The emotional toll experienced by victims of romance scams is truly devastating. The realization that one has been deceived and manipulated can result in a wide range of emotions, including betrayal, heartbreak, and profound loss. Victims may feel a deep sense of shame and embarrassment for having been taken advantage of, leading to feelings of low self-esteem and self-worth.

The psychological trauma inflicted by romance scams can have long-lasting consequences on the victims. Many individuals experience symptoms similar to those seen in post-traumatic stress disorder (PTSD), such as intrusive thoughts, flashbacks, nightmares, and hyperarousal. The trust that was once present in their relationships and interactions with others is shattered, making it difficult to form new connections or trust others in the future.

Victims often struggle with a sense of guilt and self-blame for falling victim to the scam. They may question their judgment and beat themselves up for being deceived. This self-blame can further exacerbate their emotional distress and hinder their ability to heal and move forward.

In addition to the emotional impact, romance scams also carry severe financial implications for victims. Many individuals lose significant amounts of money, sometimes their life savings or retirement funds, to these scams. The financial devastation caused by romance scams can lead to bankruptcy, foreclosure, or other serious financial hardships. Rebuilding financially after such a loss can be an arduous process that requires time, support, and professional guidance.

Coping with the aftermath of a romance scam requires both individual strength and external support. Victims are encouraged to seek out resources for emotional support, such as counseling services or therapy options. Talking to professionals who specialize in trauma recovery can help victims process their emotions, address any underlying psychological issues, and develop healthy coping mechanisms.

Self-care strategies play a crucial role in helping victims rebuild their emotional well-being. Engaging in activities that promote self-care, such as exercise, mindfulness practices, journaling, or connecting with supportive friends and family members, can aid in the healing process. It is essential for victims to prioritize their own mental and emotional well-being during this challenging time.

Moving forward from a romance scam requires a combination of reflection and growth. Victims should take the opportunity to reflect on what they have learned from the experience and how they can prevent future victimization. Building resilience and regaining self-confidence is key in forming healthy relationships again. It's important to remember that the scam was not their fault, and by seeking help and taking steps towards healing, they can reclaim their lives.

In conclusion, the emotional toll experienced by victims of romance scams is profound. The psychological trauma and long-term consequences of these scams cannot be underestimated. However, with proper support, resources, and self-care strategies, victims can begin the journey of healing and rebuilding their lives. It is crucial for society as a whole to recognize the emotional devastation caused by romance scams and provide the necessary support systems to help victims recover and move forward.

Analyzing the financial implications for victims:

Romance scams can have devastating financial consequences for their victims. Many individuals who fall prey to these scams end up losing significant amounts of money, including their savings, assets, and in some cases, even filing for bankruptcy. The scammers often manipulate their victims into giving them money through various means, such as false emergencies, promises of financial investments, or requests for travel expenses.

The financial losses suffered by victims can be substantial and have long-lasting effects on their lives. Many victims find themselves in a state of financial ruin, struggling to recover from the deceitful actions of the scammers. They may have to face the loss of their retirement funds, their homes, or other valuable possessions that they worked hard to acquire.

Additionally, the economic repercussions of romance scams extend beyond the immediate financial losses. Victims often become wary of trusting others with their money and may experience difficulty in forming new financial relationships. The trauma of being scammed can lead to feelings of vulnerability and skepticism towards financial institutions, making it challenging for victims to seek help or advice in rebuilding their financial lives.

Recovering financially after a romance scam can be a daunting task. Victims may need to work with financial advisors, lawyers, or credit counselors to regain control over their finances. It is crucial for victims to take proactive steps to address the financial aftermath of the scam, such as freezing accounts, monitoring credit reports for fraudulent activity, and reporting the crime to law enforcement agencies.

Furthermore, seeking legal recourse against the scammers may be an option for some victims. However, it is important to note that recovering stolen funds can be extremely difficult due to the complex nature of these scams and the international jurisdictional issues involved. Victims should consult with professionals who specialize in fraud cases to explore all available options.

In conclusion, the financial consequences of falling victim to a romance scam are significant and can have a profound impact on the lives of those affected. It is crucial for individuals to be aware of the warning signs and red flags associated with romance scams to avoid becoming victims themselves. Additionally, supporting and advocating for stronger regulations and enforcement against romance scams is essential to protect individuals from experiencing devastating financial losses in the future.

Understanding the psychological consequences for victims of romance scams is crucial in addressing the lasting impact of these deceptive schemes. Victims often experience a range of psychological effects, including anxiety, depression, and post-traumatic stress disorder (PTSD).

Anxiety is a common psychological consequence experienced by victims of romance scams. The betrayal and loss that come with realizing one has been deceived can lead to persistent feelings of worry, fear, and apprehension. Victims may become hypervigilant, constantly on guard for signs of deception in future relationships. This heightened state of anxiety can greatly affect a person's ability to trust others and engage in healthy emotional connections.

Depression is another psychological consequence that may occur following a romance scam. Victims often experience profound sadness, hopelessness, and a loss of interest in activities they once enjoyed. The emotional devastation caused by the scam can leave individuals feeling emotionally drained and unable to find joy or meaning in their lives. It is important to recognize and address these symptoms of depression through professional help and support.

Post-traumatic stress disorder (PTSD) is a psychological disorder that can develop after experiencing a traumatic event like a romance scam. Victims may be plagued by intrusive thoughts, nightmares, flashbacks, or intense emotional distress related to the scam. They may also avoid reminders of the incident and experience difficulties sleeping or concentrating. PTSD can have a significant impact on a person's overall well-being and quality of life, requiring specialized care and treatment.

Trust issues are a common outcome of romance scams. After being deceived by someone they believed to be their soulmate, victims often struggle to trust others, especially in romantic relationships. The breach of

80

trust experienced during the scam can make it challenging for victims to open up emotionally and establish genuine connections. Rebuilding trust takes time and support from professionals and loved ones.

Self-blame and shame are two emotions that victims often grapple with after falling victim to a romance scam. They may blame themselves for not recognizing the signs or for being too trusting. This self-blame can erode self-esteem and perpetuate feelings of shame, leaving victims hesitant to share their experiences with others or seek help. Overcoming these feelings requires self-compassion, understanding, and acceptance that anyone can fall victim to these well-crafted scams.

In conclusion, the psychological consequences of romance scams are far-reaching and can significantly impact victims' mental well-being. Understanding the effects of anxiety, depression, PTSD, trust issues, self-blame, and shame is crucial in providing appropriate support and resources for victims. It is essential for victims to seek professional help and engage in self-care strategies to navigate the complex emotional aftermath of a romance scam.

Exploring coping mechanisms and support for victims:

In the aftermath of falling victim to a romance scam, individuals often find themselves grappling with a range of intense emotions, financial hardships, and psychological distress. It is crucial for victims to seek support and guidance to navigate through these challenging circumstances.

One important avenue for support is seeking professional help through counseling services or therapy options. Speaking with a trained therapist or counselor can provide a safe space for victims to process their experiences, understand their emotions, and develop healthy coping mechanisms. These professionals can offer guidance in navigating the complex journey of healing and recovery.

Additionally, there are various resources available specifically designed to support victims of romance scams. Victims can access emotional support helplines, online support groups, and forums where they can connect with others who have had similar experiences. These platforms provide empathy, understanding, and validation, which can be instrumental in the healing process.

Self-care strategies play a vital role in rebuilding emotional well-being. Victims should prioritize self-care activities that promote relaxation, self-reflection, and personal growth. Engaging in activities such as meditation, exercise, journaling, or pursuing hobbies can help restore a sense of control and empowerment. Taking care of one's physical well-being by getting enough sleep, maintaining a healthy diet, and practicing self-compassion is also essential during this time.

It is important for victims to remember that they are not alone in their journey towards healing. Family and friends can provide crucial emotional support, lending an empathetic ear and offering comfort. Sharing one's experience with trusted loved ones can help alleviate feelings of isolation and foster a sense of belonging.

While seeking support and engaging in self-care is critical, it is equally important for victims to avoid self-blame or allowing shame to consume them. The aftermath of a romance scam can leave individuals feeling vulnerable and questioning their judgment. However, it is essential to remember that scammers are skilled manipulators who exploit vulnerabilities. Blaming oneself only reinforces the scammer's tactics and hinders the healing process.

By actively engaging in self-care practices, seeking professional help when needed, and building a supportive network, victims of romance scams can begin the journey towards healing and moving forward. It is through this process that they can regain their emotional well-being, rebuild their lives, and ultimately prevent future victimization.

Remember - healing takes time and each person's journey is unique. By being kind to yourself and reaching out for support, you are taking essential steps towards reclaiming your life after the devastating impact of a romance scam.

Practical Steps and Guidance for Recovering from the Emotional, Financial, and Psychological Fallout

Recovering from the aftermath of a romance scam can be a challenging and overwhelming process. It is essential for victims to understand that healing takes time, and everyone's journey will be unique. In this section, we will discuss practical steps and provide guidance to help victims navigate through the emotional, financial, and psychological fallout of a romance scam.

1. Seek Emotional Support:
One of the most crucial steps in the recovery process is seeking emotional support. Reach out to trusted friends, family members, or support groups who can provide a safe space for you to share your experience and emotions. Their understanding and validation can offer comfort and help in processing the trauma you've endured. Additionally, consider seeking professional help through counseling or therapy. A trained therapist can assist you in working through the complex emotions associated with the scam and provide valuable tools for healing.

2. Practice Self-Care:
Prioritize self-care as you begin to rebuild your life. Engage in activities that bring you joy, such as hobbies, exercise, or spending time with loved ones. Taking care of your physical and mental well-being is crucial during this time of healing. Nourish your body with good nutrition, get enough restful sleep, and engage in relaxation techniques like meditation or deep breathing exercises. Remember that self-care looks different for everyone, so find what works best for you.

3. Educate Yourself:
Knowledge is power when it comes to preventing future victimization. Take the opportunity to educate yourself about romance scams and their tactics. By understanding how these scams operate, you can better protect yourself and others from falling into similar traps. Stay informed about current trends in online fraud and familiarize yourself with common red flags and warning signs. Sharing your knowledge with friends or family members may also help prevent them from becoming victims themselves.

85

4. Rebuild Your Self-Confidence:

Romance scams can have a significant impact on victims' self-esteem. It is essential to remember that you were targeted because scammers saw your kindness, vulnerability, and capacity for love as strengths to exploit—not as weaknesses. Rebuilding your self-confidence starts with acknowledging your resilience and strength in overcoming this traumatic experience. Focus on your positive qualities and achievements, set achievable goals for yourself, and surround yourself with supportive people who uplift and encourage you.

5. Establish Healthy Boundaries:

After experiencing a romance scam, it is natural to feel skeptical about forming new relationships. Take the time to establish healthy boundaries when interacting with potential partners online or offline. Be cautious in sharing personal information too early in any relationship. Trust should be earned over time, rather than given freely based solely on someone's words or initial impressions. Set clear boundaries for yourself regarding financial matters, privacy, and emotional investment.

6. Learn from the Experience:

While it may be painful to reflect on the deception you experienced, it is crucial to learn from the experience to prevent future victimization. Take the time to evaluate what vulnerabilities were exploited by the scammer and how they were able to manipulate your emotions. Use this knowledge to become more discerning when engaging in online relationships moving forward. Remember that trust is earned through consistent actions over time, not just through words or gestures.

Conclusion:

Recovering from a romance scam is a journey that requires time, patience, and self-compassion. By seeking emotional support, practicing self-care, educating yourself, rebuilding your self-confidence, establishing healthy boundaries, and learning from the experience, you can reclaim your life after being deceived by a romance scammer. Remember that you are not alone in this journey, and there are resources available to support you every step of the way.

Resources for Emotional Support:

Victims of romance scams often experience a wide range of emotions, including shock, betrayal, anger, and confusion. It is crucial to acknowledge these feelings and seek emotional support during the recovery process. Many organizations and resources are available to provide assistance to individuals who have been affected by romance scams.

One valuable resource is helplines specifically dedicated to supporting scam victims. These helplines offer a listening ear, guidance, and information on available services. Trained professionals can provide emotional support, help victims navigate the aftermath of the scam, and connect them with additional resources as needed. Some helplines also have online chat options, allowing victims to seek support discreetly.

Support groups are another invaluable resource for victims of romance scams. These groups offer a safe space for individuals to share their experiences, express their emotions, and gain support from others who have gone through similar situations. Support groups can be either offline or online, with online forums providing an opportunity for anonymity if desired. Participating in support groups allows victims to find solace in knowing they are not alone and often leads to forming connections with people who truly understand their struggles.

It is important to remember that seeking professional help from therapists or counselors can greatly aid in the healing process. A trained mental health professional can guide victims through their emotions, help them develop coping strategies, and provide a framework for understanding the impact of the scam on their lives. Therapists or counselors can also assist victims in rebuilding their self-esteem and trust in others.

Online resources such as blogs, websites, and articles can also be beneficial sources of emotional support. These platforms may offer insights, stories from other survivors, and practical advice on recovering from a romance scam. Engaging with such resources can help victims gain perspective, find encouragement, and validate their experiences.

In conclusion, reaching out for emotional support is essential for victims of romance scams as they navigate the challenging process of recovery. The availability of helplines, support groups, professional counseling services, and online resources provides victims with opportunities to connect with others who have experienced similar circumstances and access the support they need to heal and move forward.

Counseling Services and Therapy Options: There is a wide range of counseling services and therapy options available to assist victims of romance scams in their healing process. These resources can provide invaluable support in addressing the emotional trauma caused by the scam.

Individual Therapy: Individual therapy is a common approach for addressing the emotional impact of a romance scam. Victims can work one-on-one with a licensed therapist who specializes in trauma, deception, or relationship issues. This therapy can help victims process their emotions, develop coping strategies, and rebuild their self-esteem and sense of trust.

Group Therapy: Group therapy offers a supportive environment where victims can connect with others who have experienced similar situations. Sharing experiences, listening to others' stories, and providing mutual support can be empowering and validating. Group therapy also provides an opportunity to learn from others' insights and coping mechanisms.

Cognitive-Behavioral Therapy (CBT): CBT is a therapeutic approach that focuses on identifying and changing negative thought patterns and behaviors. Victims of romance scams may experience self-blame, guilt, or feelings of inadequacy. CBT can help challenge these distorted thoughts, promote positive thinking, and encourage healthier behaviors.

Trauma-Focused Therapy: Trauma-focused therapy is specifically designed to address the psychological impact of traumatic experiences. It can help victims process their emotions, reduce symptoms of post-traumatic stress disorder (PTSD), and regain a sense of safety and control. This type of therapy may include techniques such as eye movement desensitization and reprocessing (EMDR) or cognitive processing therapy (CPT).

It's important for individuals seeking counseling or therapy to find professionals who have experience working with victims of scams or online deception. These professionals will have a deeper understanding of the specific dynamics involved in recovering from a romance scam.

While counseling services and therapy options are valuable tools for healing and moving forward, it's essential to remember that recovery is a unique journey for each individual. The process may take time, and it's crucial to be patient with oneself. Seeking support, guidance, and professional help can play a significant role in regaining emotional well-being and building a stronger future.

Remember, you are not alone in this journey, and there are resources available to support you. Reach out to professionals who specialize in trauma or relationship issues to explore the counseling services and therapy options that may be most beneficial to your healing process.

Practical Steps for Recovery:

To recover from the aftermath of a romance scam, victims should take practical steps to regain control of their lives and protect themselves from future scams. Here are some recommendations:

1. Establish new financial safeguards: After being scammed, it is essential to secure your finances and prevent further loss. Change your banking passwords, set up two-factor authentication for your accounts, and monitor your credit reports regularly. Consider placing a fraud alert or freeze on your credit to prevent scammers from opening accounts in your name.

2. Update online security measures: Strengthen the security of your online presence by updating passwords on all your accounts, including email addresses, social media profiles, and online banking services. Use strong and unique passwords that include a combination of letters, numbers, and symbols. Enable privacy settings on social media platforms to limit the amount of personal information scammers can access.

3. Create a self-care routine: Dealing with the aftermath of a romance scam can be emotionally draining. Establishing a self-care routine can help you heal and move forward. Set aside time each day for activities that bring you joy and relaxation, such as exercising, practicing mindfulness or meditation, journaling, or engaging in hobbies you love. Take care of your physical and mental well-being to regain your strength.

4. Engage in activities that promote healing: Find activities that promote healing and self-discovery. Consider joining support groups or online forums where you can connect with other survivors who have had similar experiences. Sharing your story and listening to others can provide validation and support during the recovery process. Engaging in creative outlets like art or writing can also help express emotions and facilitate healing.

Remember, recovery from a romance scam takes time, and everyone's healing journey is different. Be patient with yourself and seek professional help if needed. Surround yourself with understanding friends and family members who can offer support throughout the process.

By taking these practical steps, you can reclaim your life, rebuild your confidence, and protect yourself from future scams.

Rebuilding one's life and regaining confidence after falling victim to a romance scam can be a challenging journey. In this chapter, we provide guidance on how victims can navigate the path of healing and rebuilding, emphasizing the importance of setting boundaries, practicing self-compassion, and seeking support from trusted friends and family members.

One crucial aspect of rebuilding after a romance scam is setting boundaries. It's essential to establish clear limits for yourself in order to protect your emotional well-being. This may involve creating guidelines for online interactions, such as not sharing personal information too soon or being cautious about trusting others. By setting boundaries, you can regain a sense of control over your own life.

Practicing self-compassion is another vital component of the healing process. Understand that falling victim to a romance scam does not make you foolish or naive. Scammers are skilled manipulators who prey on vulnerabilities and exploit emotions. Be kind to yourself and remember that you deserve understanding and forgiveness.

Seeking support from trusted friends and family members can also play a significant role in rebuilding your life. Share your experiences with those close to you who will provide empathy and offer a listening ear. Surrounding yourself with a support system can help alleviate feelings of isolation and provide validation for your emotions.

Rebuilding trust in relationships, both online and offline, is an important goal to work towards. Take the time to heal before pursuing new romantic connections and approach future relationships with caution. Learn from the experience, be aware of red flags or warning signs, and trust your instincts. Building trust takes time, so be patient with yourself as you navigate this process.

Remember that it is possible to form healthy relationships again after experiencing a romance scam. Open communication, setting realistic expectations, and prioritizing your own well-being are key. Make sure to maintain your own interests and hobbies, as they contribute to your individual growth and happiness.

In conclusion, recovering from a romance scam is a gradual process that requires patience, self-compassion, and support from loved ones. By setting boundaries, practicing self-care, seeking support, and taking the necessary precautions in future relationships, you can rebuild your life and regain confidence. Remember that you are not alone in this journey, and there are resources available to help you along the way.

Forming healthy relationships after experiencing a romance scam is an essential part of the recovery and rebuilding process. It's crucial for victims to take time to heal before pursuing new romantic connections. Rushing into another relationship without addressing the emotional aftermath of a scam can lead to further vulnerability and potential harm.

When reentering the dating scene, it's important for victims to be vigilant and aware of potential warning signs or red flags. Learning how to spot these indicators can help protect against falling into another scam. Some common red flags include:

1. Overly fast-paced relationships: Scammers often try to establish a deep connection quickly, using love bombing techniques. Be cautious if someone is professing strong feelings or making grand promises early on in the relationship.

2. Inconsistent or evasive behavior: Pay attention to any inconsistencies in their stories, vague answers to questions, or sudden changes in behavior. Trust your instincts if something feels off.

3. Requests for money or financial assistance: Be wary of anyone who asks for financial help or tries to exploit your vulnerability. Never send money to someone you haven't met in person or have only known for a short period.

4. Lack of transparency or refusal to meet in person: If the person you're developing a relationship with hesitates or refuses to meet in person, it could be a sign that they're not genuine.

5. Pressure for personal information or access to your accounts: Be cautious if someone tries to gain access to your personal information, such

as Social Security numbers, bank account details, or passwords. Protect your privacy and only share sensitive information with trusted individuals.

To form healthy relationships moving forward, maintaining open communication is vital. Be open about your past experiences and any lingering concerns you may have. Trust and transparency are key components of a healthy relationship, so it's crucial to find someone who values these qualities.

It's also important to set realistic expectations for yourself and future partners. Understand that trust may take time to rebuild and that it's okay to take things slow. Take the opportunity to learn from past mistakes and use them as lessons for establishing healthy boundaries in future relationships.

Prioritizing your own well-being is essential in forming healthy relationships after experiencing a romance scam. Take care of yourself emotionally, mentally, and physically. Engage in self-care activities that promote healing and self-discovery. Surround yourself with a supportive network of friends and family who can provide encouragement and understanding.

Remember that healing takes time, and it's essential to be patient with yourself during this process. By being vigilant, maintaining open communication, setting realistic expectations, prioritizing your well-being, and learning from past experiences, you can form healthy relationships and prevent future scams.

In conclusion, forming healthy relationships after experiencing a romance scam requires taking time to heal, being vigilant for warning signs, practicing open communication, setting realistic expectations, prioritizing well-being, and learning from past experiences. By implementing these strategies, victims can move forward with confidence and resilience in their quest for genuine love and companionship.

Prevention and Global Efforts: Combating the Romance Scam

Various global initiatives have been established to combat the pervasive issue of romance scams. These initiatives range from organizations and agencies dedicated to addressing the problem to task forces specifically focused on tackling this form of cybercrime.

One prominent organization is the International Consumer Protection and Enforcement Network (ICPEN), which brings together consumer protection authorities from around the world. ICPEN works to promote cooperation among its members and shares information to combat scams, including romance scams, on an international scale. The organization aims to raise awareness, enhance enforcement efforts, and educate the public about the risks associated with online fraud.

Additionally, law enforcement agencies, such as Interpol and the Federal Bureau of Investigation (FBI), play a crucial role in combating romance scams. These agencies work tirelessly to investigate and apprehend the individuals behind these scams, often operating across borders to bring offenders to justice. Their efforts contribute to dismantling criminal networks and preventing further victimization.

Task forces have also been established at both national and international levels. For example, the United States has the Internet Crime Complaint Center (IC3), a partnership between the FBI and the National White Collar Crime Center (NW3C). IC3 serves as a central repository for complaints related to cybercrimes, including romance scams, and facilitates collaboration between law enforcement agencies.

In addition to these organizations, private companies in the tech industry are taking steps to address romance scams. Dating websites and social media platforms are implementing measures to detect and remove fraudulent profiles, employing advanced algorithms and machine learning techniques. Some platforms also provide resources and educational materials to help users recognize and avoid potential scams.

Prevention strategies are vital in the fight against romance scams Individuals can protect themselves by being cautious when engaging in online relationships. It is essential to remain vigilant while interacting with others, especially on dating websites and social media platforms. Recognizing common red flags, such as requests for money or personal information early on, can help individuals avoid falling victim to scams.

Awareness campaigns are another powerful tool in combatting romance scams. These campaigns aim to educate the public about the tactics used by scammers and highlight the importance of maintaining privacy and security online. By raising awareness about the risks associated with online relationships, these campaigns empower individuals to make informed decisions and protect themselves from potential scams.

Educational programs targeting various age groups and demographics are also crucial in preventing romance scams. Schools, community centers, and online platforms can implement comprehensive programs that teach individuals how to recognize potential scammer behaviors, understand online risks, and promote digital literacy. By equipping people with knowledge and skills, these educational programs contribute to creating a more resilient population against romance scams.

In conclusion, global initiatives aimed at combating romance scams have been established through organizations, law enforcement agencies, task forces, private companies, awareness campaigns, and educational programs. These efforts tackle different aspects of the issue, such as investigation and enforcement, prevention strategies, raising awareness, and promoting education. By working together at various levels, we can effectively address this insidious crime and protect individuals from falling victim to romance scams.

Prevention strategies for combating romance scams involve educating individuals on how to recognize and avoid potential scammers. By implementing these strategies and maintaining online privacy and security, individuals can significantly reduce their risk of falling victim to a romance scam.

One important prevention strategy is to be cautious when communicating with someone online. It is essential to be aware that scammers often use fake profiles and stolen identities to create an illusion of trustworthiness. To protect yourself, take the following precautions:

1. Stay vigilant: Maintain a healthy level of skepticism when interacting with someone online, especially if they show signs of being too good to be true. Remember that scammers often prey on vulnerability and emotional needs.

2. Verify their identity: Use search engines and social media platforms to research the person you are communicating with. Look for inconsistencies in their stories or images that appear elsewhere online. If something feels off, trust your instincts.

3. Protect personal information: Be cautious about sharing personal information, such as your home address, financial details, or social security number. Scammers may use this information for identity theft or other fraudulent activities.

4. Use secure communication channels: When communicating with someone online, consider using secure messaging apps or platforms that offer encryption. This can help safeguard your conversations from potential hackers or scammers.

5. Be wary of requests for money: One common tactic used by romance scammers is to ask their victims for money under various pretexts, such as medical emergencies or travel expenses. Never send money to someone you have never met in person.

Safe online dating practices are also crucial in preventing romance scams. Follow these guidelines:

1. Choose reputable dating websites and platforms: Select dating websites and social media platforms that have strict policies in place to detect and remove fraudulent profiles. Research the platform's safety features and read reviews from other users before creating an account.

2. Take it slow: Develop relationships gradually, taking the time to get to know someone before becoming emotionally invested. Scammers often try to rush the relationship and push for personal or financial commitments early on.

3. Trust your intuition: If something feels off or too good to be true, trust your gut feeling. Don't ignore warning signs or red flags, even if you feel a strong emotional connection with the person.

By implementing these prevention strategies and safe online dating practices, individuals can significantly reduce their risk of falling victim to a romance scam. Awareness and vigilance are key in protecting yourself and your loved ones from the devastating consequences of this form of cybercrime.

Awareness campaigns play a crucial role in combating romance scams by raising public awareness about the issue and educating individuals about the tactics used by scammers. These campaigns aim to empower people with knowledge, enabling them to recognize and avoid potential scams.

The significance of awareness campaigns cannot be overstated. By increasing awareness, individuals become more vigilant and are less likely to fall victim to romance scams. They learn to identify red flags, such as inconsistencies in stories, requests for money or personal information, and excessive declarations of love at an early stage of an online relationship. The goal is to encourage individuals to trust their instincts and take necessary precautions when interacting with others online.

Successful awareness campaigns have been implemented worldwide, utilizing various channels and platforms to reach a wide audience. These campaigns leverage the power of social media, television commercials, radio announcements, posters, and educational materials distributed in schools, libraries, and community centers. The messaging is designed to resonate with different demographics, highlighting the emotional and financial consequences of falling victim to a romance scam.

To ensure the effectiveness of awareness campaigns, it is important to consider the following suggestions:

1. Collaborate with reputable organizations: Partnering with established organizations specializing in cybersecurity, fraud prevention, or victim support can lend credibility to the campaign. These organizations can provide valuable expertise and resources to create engaging content that resonates with the target audience.

2. Craft compelling messages: The messaging should be informative, relatable, and easily understandable. It should emphasize the emotional impact of romance scams, while also providing practical tips for avoiding them. Using real-life stories and testimonials from survivors can help make the message more relatable and impactful.

3. Utilize multiple communication channels: To reach a broad range of individuals, the campaign should utilize various communication channels. This could include social media platforms, television and radio advertisements, online forums and communities, public events, and collaborations with influencers or celebrities who can help spread the message.

4. Tailor outreach methods for different demographics: Different age groups and demographics may respond better to specific outreach methods. For example, younger audiences may be more receptive to social media campaigns, while older adults may prefer educational workshops or printed materials. Tailoring outreach methods ensures that the campaign reaches its intended audience effectively.

By implementing effective awareness campaigns, individuals can be educated about the tactics used by romance scammers and empowered to protect themselves and their loved ones. These campaigns not only raise public awareness but also contribute to the overall prevention of romance scams by creating a culture of vigilance and informed decision-making.

In conclusion, awareness campaigns are instrumental in combating romance scams. By raising public awareness and providing individuals with the necessary knowledge to recognize and avoid scams, these campaigns play a vital role in preventing individuals from becoming victims. By collaborating with reputable organizations, crafting compelling messages, utilizing multiple communication channels, and tailoring outreach methods for different demographics, these campaigns can have a significant impact on reducing the prevalence of romance scams.

This section of "Anatomy of the Romance Scam" discusses the importance of educational programs in preventing romance scams. These programs play a crucial role in equipping individuals with the knowledge and awareness necessary to recognize the red flags and risks associated with online relationships.

Comprehensive educational programs targeting different age groups and demographics are essential in addressing this issue effectively. Schools, community centers, and online platforms should implement these educational initiatives to reach a wide audience.

One key aspect of these programs is teaching individuals to recognize red flags that may indicate a romance scam. By understanding the tactics used by scammers, such as love bombing, mirroring, and gaslighting, individuals can better protect themselves from falling victim to these deceitful schemes.

Educational programs should also focus on promoting digital literacy and online safety. This includes teaching individuals about the potential risks and vulnerabilities associated with online interactions, as well as providing guidance on maintaining privacy and security settings on various platforms.

By enhancing digital literacy, individuals can navigate online relationships with a greater level of caution and skepticism. They will be empowered to distinguish between genuine connections and manipulative tactics employed by scammers.

In conclusion, comprehensive educational programs are vital in combating romance scams. By educating individuals about the red flags, risks, and strategies employed by scammers, these programs equip people with the tools needed to prevent falling victim to these deceptive schemes. Through increased awareness and digital literacy, we can collectively work towards the eradication of romance scams.

Calls to Action: Taking a Stand Against Romance Scams

The battle against romance scams requires the collective efforts of individuals, communities, law enforcement agencies, and governments. By recognizing the severity and impact of these scams, we can work together to prevent future victims and hold scammers accountable. This section concludes our exploration of prevention and global efforts by outlining specific steps that can be taken at various levels to combat the romance scam epidemic.

At an individual level, awareness and education are key. It is crucial for individuals to familiarize themselves with the signs and red flags of romance scams. By staying informed, individuals can protect themselves and spread awareness among their friends and family. It is also important to maintain a healthy skepticism when engaging in online relationships, especially when encountering suspicious behavior or requests for money or personal information. Sharing experiences and stories can empower others to recognize potential scams and avoid becoming victims.

Communities also play a vital role in combating romance scams. Local organizations, community centers, schools, and religious institutions can organize awareness campaigns and educational programs on the dangers of romance scams. By partnering with law enforcement agencies and experts in cybersecurity, these organizations can provide resources, support, and guidance to those vulnerable to scams. Together, communities can foster a culture of caution and vigilance when it comes to online relationships.

Law enforcement agencies have a critical role in investigating and prosecuting romance scammers. These agencies should allocate adequate resources and manpower to tackle this issue effectively. Enhanced collaboration between local authorities, national agencies, and international organizations can lead to efficient identification, apprehension, and prosecution of scammers. By sharing intelligence, leveraging technology, and implementing robust investigation techniques, law enforcement agencies can make significant headway in dismantling scamming operations.

Governments must also prioritize the fight against romance scams by enacting comprehensive legislation. Laws should be established to combat online fraud specifically related to romantic relationships. This includes criminalizing the act of perpetrating romance scams, imposing strict penalties for offenders, and providing legal recourse for victims. Governments should invest in the training of law enforcement personnel to better equip them in investigating these complex cybercrimes. Additionally, cooperation between countries is crucial for extraditing offenders across borders and fostering international cooperation against romance scams.

International collaboration through forums, conferences, and task forces is essential in exchanging best practices and strategies for combating romance scams. Agencies such as Interpol and Europol have already taken steps towards addressing this issue globally. Moreover, partnerships with private sector entities, including dating websites and social media platforms, are crucial in enhancing security measures and providing swift response mechanisms for users who fall prey to scams.

In conclusion, combatting the romance scam epidemic requires a multi-faceted approach involving individuals, communities, law enforcement agencies, and governments. By raising awareness, educating ourselves and those around us, supporting victims, enhancing law enforcement efforts, strengthening legislation, and fostering international cooperation, we can work together to dismantle this insidious crime. Let us take a stand against romance scams and create a safer digital landscape where love can flourish without fear of exploitation.

Author Bio:

I once had an ugly and expensive habit. I was too small for robbery, so I learned to scam. I scammed millions of dollars over the years. However, my life took a turn for the better, and I am now clean and serene for many years. Retiring from the corporate world, I now dedicate my time to rebuilding the destruction I once caused.

Through this informative non-fiction book series, podcasts, YouTube channel (@CaTomCatt), and nationwide seminars, I aim to share my personal experience-based knowledge to help others protect themselves against scams. Drawing from my past as a scammer, I bring a unique perspective to this important topic by delving into the technical tactics, scientific facts, and data-driven insights behind various types of scams.

As someone who has been on both sides of the scamming spectrum, I understand the devastating consequences that falling for a scam can have on individuals and society as a whole. My goal with this series is to empower readers with the tools and knowledge they need to defeat common scams using common sense.

By examining the anatomy of scams, uncovering the psychological techniques employed by scammers, and providing practical advice on recognizing red flags and taking action, I hope to equip readers with the skills necessary to protect themselves and their loved ones.

Join me on this journey of scam prevention and together, let's foster a culture of skepticism and critical thinking that will discourage scammers from preying on innocent victims. With awareness, education, and a reliance on common sense, we can overcome the threat of scams and create a safer digital landscape for all.

I invite you to dive into Volume 1 of "Scammer! Defeat common scams with Common Sense!" where we explore the understanding of scams, how they operate, the psychology behind successful scams, spotting red flags, responding to scams, reporting scams, recovering from a scam, supporting friends falling for scams, and much more. Together, let's use our collective knowledge and experiences to outsmart scammers and protect ourselves from their deceptive tactics.

Stay tuned for the next Volume of "Defeat common scams with Common Sense!" where we will explore advanced scam defense techniques and dive even deeper into the world of scams, fraud prevention, and recovery. Together, let's continue our journey of scam awareness, education, and empowerment.

The author:

Hon. Thomas Mitchell, DD, PhD
Lord of Kerry, Republic of Ireland
Knight, Order of Minerva